WITHIN THESE STREETS

WITHIN THESE
STREETS

JAMES CARRÉ-RICE

ISBN: 978-1-976524-25-7

Editorial & Design Services: The Write Factor
www.thewritefactor.co.uk

To the power of hope

CONTENTS

ACKNOWLEDGEMENTS

For the loving belief and
encouragement of my wife, Jacqueline

For the skilled professionalism of Lorna Howarth,
my Editor from The Write Factor

And for the living, loving power of 'life' itself,
that broke me free from the destructive personality
in which I was once hopelessly lost

Also by James Carré-Rice

Another Kind of Knowing

PROLOGUE

...welcome to my book...it's hard to believe that 25 years have passed since i wrote the original, and of course, a huge amount has changed since that time...

...the first edition was primarily aimed at young male prisoners, and therefore written in a pacey fashion that might best grab their attention...

however, it was a thrill to see it become popular with people from all walks of life...

...in order to distribute as many copies as possible throughout the prison systems of the UK, US and Canada, i took no royalty payments...and a charity was formed to pay for printing and distribution...

...along with the story itself, the message contained within these pages is one of hope... no matter how stuck you may feel, or the mess your life may be in, keys exist that will break the deadlock and open the doors...

...in the midst of my darkest hours i once sat at a kitchen table and said, almost in a daydream, "i'll figure this out one day"...and i did...i also knew that if i could do it, i'd help a great many people to do the same...and that also came true...

...if any of my words and experiences resonate with you, take hold of them, treasure them and make something happen...

...you know, i've noticed something quite amazing about life...if we genuinely search for answers, it's as if a door gets kicked, causing it to stand slightly ajar, not quite open...and if we pass through it, no matter how small or innocuous the opportunity... it leads to another door being kicked ajar...

...but remember...they are your personal doors and nobody can pass through them for you...

...you will notice as you read that i have written short commentaries along the way...they are my current observations on my life as it was back then...

...now, the longest journey has to begin with the first footstep, so let's get started...

CHAPTER 1

Running Wild

I was dragged out of sleep by a big hand ripping at my collar, a hammer raised to strike and two bulging eyes staring into mine. I just hoped in that split-second he'd recognise me.

"James! What are you doing here?" asked Uncle Jack, loosening his grip and lowering the hammer.

"I've run away," came the answer, fright squirting the truth straight out of my mouth.

"Come on lad," he said, lumbering his thick frame across the back yard of his terraced house.

I grabbed my things and followed, wondering what his reaction might be. He'd always been my favorite uncle but running away might be pushing things a bit far.

I'd arrived home late the previous night to find my dad's house locked and in darkness. Dreading a telling off, I'd knocked tentatively, almost hoping not to be heard. After four attempts, I remembered that he'd been taking sleeping tablets following a recent car crash and was unlikely to hear a thing. As I stood on the doorstep, the gathering cold reminded me of the long uncomfortable night ahead, but unbeknown to me, something far worse than that was afoot; the toughest ten years of my life were about to unfold, and I'd be lucky to survive them.

My mind wandered back over the recent years leading up to my parents' divorce. After starting secondary school aged 11, my behaviour, which had always been fairly boisterous, deteriorated. My academic progress was stifled by my rebellious attitude and constant arguing. I was more interested in making a name for myself than doing as I was told. I often felt carried along by a river of bad behaviour and it was only when severely confronted and asked to explain myself that I realised I didn't know why I was conducting myself in such a way.

"Why did you punch that boy/break that window/smash that bottle…?"

"I don't know," I'd say, standing there looking dumb.

It was easy to get hold of strong drink and I loved the wild abandon it gave me. However, the aggression it sparked caused my friends to become increasingly wary of me, especially when I drank at school. Eventually my behaviour reached a point where I was barred from all my classes and forced to learn in isolation.

Before long, my mother took my brother, sister and I to live in an unfamiliar place along the banks of the River Mersey. Moving to a new area was hard for all of us. I hated it. My new school was scruffy and less disciplined than the previous one, but the slack rules provided room for me to flex my restless personality. While my mother struggled with social security problems, along with the emotional upheaval of leaving my dad, I got my kicks out on the streets. With my father out of the way I often skipped school, stayed out late at night and hung out with a rough local gang.

After being involved in a large drunken brawl one evening, I was arrested and locked up by the police. Still aged 14 and classed as a juvenile, a guardian was required to come and collect me. News that my dad was on his way instead of my mum sobered me up in double-quick time. I sat in the cell anxiously awaiting the confrontation, but to my surprise he reacted calmly and had little to say. In fact, he offered me a cigarette on the way home. It felt weird smoking in front of him but a better atmosphere developed between us. Later that night he asked whether I'd like to move back to live with him, but I agreed more out of politeness than genuine desire. I was very confused and constantly wrestled with uncontrollable urges.

Just two weeks later, there I stood on his doorstep, kicking my heels in the cold. It suited me to believe he'd locked me out deliberately, offering a good excuse to cut loose and run away. My little tale of rejection would deflect the blame nicely onto my dad while drumming up sympathy for me. I liked a bit of sympathy. As I crept around the back of the house to break in and collect some things, my emotions rocked upon a seesaw of excitement and fear. Entering an upstairs window proved extremely difficult, but once inside another dilemma faced me. There before me stood the bed I'd slept in for years; I need only climb in and sleep, putting an end to the quandary.

The light of common sense exposed the fabrication of my self-pitying story, but quickly and aggressively I suppressed those feelings, snatched up a few of my belongings and disappeared. The full impact of what I was doing hit me as I walked along those long empty streets. Many anguished tears rolled down my face as the pain of separation gripped me in a way I hadn't expected.

"What have I done?" I asked myself again and again.

The light of new hope kept my legs moving despite the intrusion of a thousand burning thoughts, and after three hours I stood outside my destination. Uncle Jack had a disused car inside the lock-up at the end of his back yard. I could rest there for a few hours and be gone before he woke up in the morning. Breaking in was easy enough, but once inside I found it intolerably cold, smelly and uncomfortable.

Sleep seemed impossible but somehow, shivering and tired, I dropped off while sitting upright.

◆ ◆ ◆

Smelling fusty like the old car, I now sat feeling exhausted while Uncle Jack talked to me through the open door to the kitchen while peeling spuds. He thought chips would be a great idea for breakfast and set to work cooking them while I, hardly feeling able to refuse, dreaded their arrival.

Following years of illness, Uncle Jack lived alone. Periods locked up in hospitals followed violent incidents that were 'kept from little ears.'

"Your Uncle Jack's not well son," was all I ever heard.

During our conversation, my ears pricked up when I heard him say, 'I'll get you a job on the site with me, lad."

"Thanks Uncle Jack," I replied, genuinely surprised.

I played it cool but deep down inside my heart leapt at this sudden upturn in fortunes. All being well, I'd have a place to hide and a job – and I wasn't being packed off to school. It wasn't the glittering start I'd imagined, but it would serve to make my family realise that I wasn't about to come crying home.

The warmth of the heater drew out my tiredness into a string of yawns, filling my eyes with tears as the chips arrived with a bottle of brown sauce. I struggled through enough of them to satisfy Uncle Jack then, and with my immediate worries over, fell fast asleep.

The following morning Jack had me up early, running bleary eyed through the dark streets to catch a bus. Despite appearing much older than my fourteen years and clearly dressed for work, Uncle Jack insisted on paying half fare. The conductor reluctantly surrendered to Jack's menacing appearance without a word while I stared out of the window, embarrassed. Arriving on site, I was given the job of 'can lad,' (tea-maker) by the grumpy boss whose attitude flattened all possibility of enthusiasm. Setting about my duties, I reflected upon the rude awakening my romantic idea of running away had received. However, it was the freedom to hang out late at night with my friends that made it all worthwhile. Tearing around the streets with them was the main attraction for leaving home in the first place.

There were many kids who hung around each day instead of going to school, while others showed up at night to see what was going on. The nearby shopping precinct was the hub of activity; all the shops had their windows boarded up and covered in graffiti. A seedy nightclub was situated in the middle of it all, owned by an American guy, and it was a miracle how he kept his licence; there were fights inside and out almost every night. The prostitutes who brought sailors from the docks gave us cigarettes and money on the way in. We were always hanging around, sometimes picking up valuables dropped in scuffles or trying to part a drunk from his money.

The area was always filled with colorful characters at night, and you had the feeling anything could happen. I envied those whose poor upbringing allowed a type of behaviour I'd never been permitted. With little concept of the true misery of their lives, I wanted to be associated with their rough identity and enjoy the fruit of indiscipline. Despite equipping myself with a good excuse for running away and being willing to play my part in the late-night escapades, it was a rough district where acceptance wasn't guaranteed.

One particular night at a local disco, I had a few dances with a girl I liked, but unfortunately, she had a boyfriend called Jonah, a guy I didn't know. Donna liked me and confessed she wanted to get rid of Jonah:

"He's always with his stupid mates," she said. "He never bothers with me."

Later when everybody spilled out into the precinct, others drifted in to mix with us from nearby streets. The atmosphere bounced with shouts, whistles, singing, shouting, smoking and laughter, but then suddenly one of Donna's friends tugged my sleeve.

"Jonah's here with his mates," she said. "You'd better clear off in case he starts."

I didn't like the idea of being frightened-off, but the warmth I'd previously enjoyed as part of the crowd had now become punctuated with steely looks. Feeling unsure, I drew heavily on my cigarette before stepping aside to leave, but suddenly my head exploded and the world spun around as I felt myself being dragged across the pavement by the hair. The crowd jostled noisily for position amid screaming girls as I grappled furiously to get a grip on my attacker.

We wrestled, kicked, banged heads and punched furiously until finally I broke myself free, knocked Jonah to the ground and started beating him. A figure darted from the crowd and kicked me, followed by a few others until I fell unconscious to the floor. Meanwhile, scuffles broke out among the crowd and girls fought with those who'd been kicking me, but by then I was in a complete daze.

I regained consciousness leaning against the wall of a nearby alleyway; an echoing voice became that of a girl trying to hold me up. She'd apparently helped me stagger away as the police arrived with their truncheons in hand, ready to split a few heads. Lighting a cigarette for me she related what had happened. It was clear that I'd beaten Jonah before the attack by his mates, but instead of seeking revenge, I looked forward to the increased credibility the fight was sure to bring.

After two weeks, I was laid off from the job, which suited me just fine – I'd rather be out on the streets with my mates. We wandered around causing trouble, stealing, smashing things up, fighting, tattooing one-another and generally causing a rumpus everywhere we went.

Arriving home late one night, I found Uncle Jack sitting waiting for me in a state of agitation.

"That feller around the back is giving me fuckin' trouble," he said, his eyes ablaze.

"Which feller?' I asked.

"That bald-headed twat with the van," he answered. "We're going to sort him out, big style."

I couldn't understand what the problem was, and suspected that it may have been all in his head; the turmoil in his eyes was there for anyone to see. Luckily, I managed to talk him out of a violent attack; instead we crept out in the middle of the night and hammered six-inch nails into all four tyres of his van.

Over the weeks that followed I drifted away from Uncle Jack's, preferring instead to stay with the crowd I was meeting in the pubs. The older guys were different from my mates and had given up hanging around street corners looking for the next fight. Instead they liked to drink in comfort, buy decent drugs, waltz in and out of nightclubs and breeze through life in the easiest way possible. Occasionally, they ended up without money, but information would soon arrive about a lucrative job to pull off. It was common to pay shop staff to take a walk for five minutes while expensive equipment got carried away.

During that period, I met up with Denny, an old school friend who was fascinated by all the things I'd been getting up to since running away. The gang made him welcome, sharing ciggies, money and drink before he'd catch his bus home each night. Despite the lax pub rules, Denny didn't look old enough to get served, so we had to sneak him in through a back window and keep him hidden.

I was pretty selfish in those days and soon grew tired of having to accommodate his younger looks and lack of 'street cred'. He was getting in the way of my big plans. Therefore, I began avoiding him, letting him wander around the streets alone until he eventually gave up and stopped visiting. I felt bad about this, but I reckoned I'd soon forget him, just like I had my family. I didn't want to be tied down by the needs of others.

Following a few close shaves with the police, I was arrested and locked up again. When my mother arrived to collect me, my head dropped in dismay, knowing the further grief I was bringing to her.

Riding home in the taxi, she tried to cheer me up, but I remained impassive and wouldn't let her near me. I no longer believed I had any right to her love and couldn't be bothered with all the complications of family life.

"Why can't you just forget me?" I'd say. "Just leave me alone, I'm no good for you anymore."

My harsh words and actions were intended to push her to the brink and force her to reject me so that we could both be free.

"You'll have your own kids one day. Then you'll see," she said, repeating a phrase I was getting sick of hearing.

While waiting to attend court, I was ordered to live at her house and go back to school. Despite enjoying some aspects of home life, I found conflicts increasingly hard to deal with and soon ran away again.

Thus began a pattern of behaviour that repeated itself many times over subsequent years.

I went to a number of schools while living with a succession of relatives following various arrests. Despite my outward toughness, my over-sensitivity at home began shaping my behaviour out on the streets. Moving from one gang to another, drifting from girl to girl, never wanting to commit myself to anybody or anything.

Things came to a head one night when, having taken a cocktail of drugs and alcohol, I arrived home and started shouting at my new step-father. Fearing what may happen, my mother was forced to call the police. I hated my mum's feller – he seemed like a big phony to me and I was itching to prove it. Nevertheless, I left calmly with the police and stood chatting with them further along the street.

"Come on, sunshine," one of them said. "We don't want to arrest you. You've just had an argument, that's all. Now, why don't you go back, say you're sorry and everything will calm down."

"Okay, I will," I said. "Thanks."

As they climbed back into their police car, I picked up a large rock and smashed it into one of their doors. We wrestled all the way to the police cells and I came off second-best. They locked me up for the night and made sure I'd be up before the Magistrates the following day.

My dad met me at the court where we sat waiting in a long corridor with shiny floors. People stood around murmuring in small groups, wearing ill-fitting suits and worried expressions. Suddenly, through the haze of cigarette smoke and clicking footsteps on the marble tiles I could hear my name being called by the Usher.

"Rice – do we have a James Rice?"

We stood up.

"This must be it then," gulped my dad.

A ruddy-faced man in a black gown approached carrying a bundle of papers. "Are you James Rice?" he barked, for all to hear.

"Yes, I am."

"Then you'd better take these," he said, leafing charge sheets into my hands, one after the other: "Rice, Rice, Rice, Rice…"

I quickly glanced through them, recognising each wild incident with a shudder. "Oh shit," I thought.

With hardly a moment to prepare, we were called in and once the opening formalities were over, the Prosecutor began reading out the offences. Hearing them presented in such stark terms was like being undressed in public. I became painfully aware of my father standing just yards away, listening to it all.

What would the Magistrates think of this wild, drunken, abusive and violent creature standing before them? I dreaded to think. My plea of, 'Guilty as charged' was the signal for much flapping in outrage among the Magistrates. Things looked bad. After my dad spoke a few words in my defence, they calmed down a little bit, but no sooner had he sat down, than the Clerk was on his feet pecking at the Magistrates with stern advice in hushed tones.

The fat man in the middle raised his hand, called for order and spoke. "Young man, there has to be some recompense for your behaviour…"

I held my breath as he paused, doing my best to look as innocent as possible.

"We have no alternative but to sentence you to three months in a Detention Center. Take him away."

My legs almost turned to jelly as I was led down the steps. Three months didn't sound like much if you said it quickly, but the weight of it was suddenly killing me.

"What a wimp I really am," I thought.

My pockets were emptied, forms signed and handcuffs placed on my wrists for the four-hour trip into the unknown. Looking out through the windows as we sped along in the police van, I wished with all my heart I could be somebody else; I hated my life.

◆ ◆ ◆

The safe haven of the journey ended all too soon as the van pulled up outside two large brown gates. The whole place seemed unnaturally quiet as we passed through a series of locked doors that led to the reception area. An officer appeared with a friendly smile and asked my name.

"Jimmy," I replied.

Smack! My head spun. He'd hit me hard across the face. A rage boiled inside me.

"You call me 'sir'. Don't ever forget."

I wouldn't, but deep in my heart I wanted to kill him. The police officers looked embarrassed handing me over into care of the Detention Centre and once the paperwork was completed they left without a word.

I was gripped with fear, feeling threatened in the hands of my captors. 'Anything could happen to me here,' I thought. By keeping my mouth shut I made it through the reception procedure without any further fuss. I was locked in a tiny cell to wait while other prisoners were brought through the gate. Meanwhile, my mind wandered back to my old school where even at that very moment they might be doing English or perhaps sports on the playing field. The thought of it was almost unbearable, but I held the emotion back. 'Why couldn't I have stuck with school?' I wondered. 'Why am I so bad?' My old life seemed like a million miles away, lost forever.

Later, I was led to an enormous dining room filled with prisoners who stared while I was shown to my seat. I took an instant dislike to the one sat opposite me, who probed me with stupid questions.

"Where are you from? What are you in for?"

I was too deep within myself to be bothered answering him and ended up telling him to, "Shut your fucking face."

Long before dark, four of us were led to small cells and locked up for our first night. As newcomers, we would have to sleep alone in small cells for a few nights before being allocated to dormitories. As the door locked shut, the walls seemed to close in and suffocate me. With my freedom gone, I suffered a terrible emptiness that was almost unbearable – and that was just the first night. I wanted to cry out but held everything inside. Instead, I began to think of happier days, of times with my brother and sister, both of whose innocence ensured their comfort and security within family life.

"Why have I gone this way?" I wondered. "Why can't I accept a simple life?'"

It was an endless night with little sleep, unhappy thoughts, and an absolute dread of the morning.

The following day proved equally eventful, beginning with a visit to the Governor who told me I'd only have to serve six weeks of the sentence if I behaved myself, otherwise I'd be kept in for the entire three months. It sounded like good news, but even six weeks seemed interminable for me. I hated every moment of it with a passion.

After that, we were set to work scrubbing floors on our hands and knees for the entire day. No talking or smoking was allowed, which made it drag all the more. Before supper we were taken to a canteen (prison shop) to be given advance pay. Nobody was allowed to have cash, but we were given goods to the value of our earnings. While we were waiting lined up in the corridor, another work party arrived and stood nearby while our officer disappeared for a chat with somebody. One of the lads from the other party turned to me and asked, "What are you in for, dickhead?"

I couldn't believe my ears. "You what?" I answered, angrily.

"Oh, he's getting upset now," he said, laughing to his friends.

Somehow, he seemed to think there was no danger in what he was saying. With little sense of the rules or the consequences that may fall upon me, I punched him hard in the face and he fell to the ground. At that moment, the prison doctor turned into the corridor and saw me standing over the lad, a big commotion stirring all around.

"Who did that? What's going on?" he asked in a panic.

"I did it," I said. "He…" I wanted to explain that he had started it, but the doctor pressed an alarm bell on the wall and wouldn't listen. The stupid lad lay on the floor as a group of officers charged at me, grabbed both of my arms and dragged me away into the punishment block for a spell of solitary confinement.

An hour later I was ordered out of the cell and marched into a room where I was to face the Governor for the second time that day. They stood me on a slippery mat to prevent me gaining any purchase in the event I attacked anybody. Two officers stood in front of me protecting the Governor, who sat behind a large desk.

The Chief Officer, a rotund man, barked at me, "Rice, you are charged with assaulting prisoner Baker. How do you plead, guilty or not guilty?"

I couldn't believe this. It was like being back in court. "Well, the thing is…" I began, but he cut me off.

"Guilty or not guilty?" he snapped loudly.

"Well, it's just that…"

This time his face turned purple as he shouted, "Did you do it or not?"

"Yes, sir," I said, resigned to the outcome.

The Governor scribbled notes while the fat Chief Officer whispered and the two officers in front of me stared. It all seemed slightly unreal. Then the Governor spoke.

"Rice, you've come here with a bad record, but we won't accept your violent behaviour. You'll spend seven days in solitary confinement; lose three weeks' pay and three days remission. Do you understand?"

I didn't, but said, "Yes, sir," and was then quickly marched back to that bare cell.

The punishment block was much tougher than the rest of the place, a mixture of painful isolation, grueling work and punishing workouts in the gym. My physical strength and skill with a ball helped me get along with the gym staff, but didn't excuse me from some of their nasty games. I was often placed in the basketball circle in the middle of the gym, then one lad from each end was sent in to try and fight me out of it. Many made only feeble attempts while others really had a go, but I bounced them all out of my circle every time; the punishment block officer loved it when I hurt somebody.

The first good feelings I enjoyed in that place came on the day I was allowed to go back to the normal regime. The rest of the place seemed easy compared to where I'd been for a week. It was about then that I started to notice how young many of the other prisoners seemed, despite us all being a similar age. There were some obviously 'bad' ones, but I couldn't imagine how many of the others had ever reached a Detention Centre – they looked permanently bewildered and a few of them cried at night.

A lad called Ginger, who spoke like a little posh school-boy, was probably the most out of place. He reacted wrongly to everything on account of his nerves and giggled when bullies snapped at him, which infuriated them even more. When an officer bawled at him one day for not scrubbing a floor properly, he laughed and told him not to be so silly. I couldn't believe my ears. The officer went berserk, kicked his bucket all over the floor and made him scrub it all over again.

Eventually, I was moved to a dormitory that I had to share with twenty other lads; it was like a hospital ward without the frills. Ginger approached as I unrolled my kit onto the bed,

"You'll have to do a dorm run tonight, Ricey," he said. "Everybody has to."

16

"What's a dorm run?" I asked without looking up.

"You have to climb over one bed and then under the next, all the way around the dorm while everybody hits you with pillowcases filled with boots and things."

"And who's gonna make me do that?" I asked, feeling myself stiffen in aggression.

"Dawson," he said. "He's the boss of the dorm." As the room started to fill with prisoners, Ginger pointed him out.

"He can do mine for me," I said.

Ginger disappeared looking excited while I sat quietly on my bed, and sure enough, Dawson made his approach.

"You new then?"

"No, I've been in the block," I answered without looking at him.

"You'll have to do a dorm run you know, everybody does." He didn't order me like he might some of the others, more a request.

"You can do mine, pal," I said.

"Wh, what!" he said, trying to smile and keep things light.

"You can do mine," I repeated, this time standing up and staring into his face. "I'm not doing any fucking dorm run, so go on, fuck off."

He backed-off quickly, crushed by the situation and tried to do his best to look cool, but he was finished. His personal dominion over the dorm had ended right there and then. The other lads quickly found out that I wasn't exactly a newcomer, but had been kept in the punishment block for fighting.

I paid no interest in bullying anybody and wouldn't allow it in the dormitory; I just wanted to get through my sentence the easiest way possible. Over the weeks that followed, Dawson started to pay the price for the bullying he'd done. Knowing that I'd protect them, the other lads exacted their revenge upon him in all sorts of ways until eventually, the screws had to move him out.

17

Following the harsh regime of each day, the period between supper and sleep was often filled with the excited chatter of relief. Some read books or wrote letters home, while others curled up on their beds, riddled with the pain of homesickness. We all missed the families we had so easily taken for granted. However, there were plenty of others who had become institutionalised after placements in strings of children's homes, usually as a result of neglectful parenting. It was hard to imagine how they would ever break out of their downhill spiral; they seemed to be steeped in a mentality of incarceration.

Release day was always tantalisingly elusive, so near but so painfully far away, but despite the endless grind, my last night soon arrived. I felt like a rich man, in possession of the one thing everybody craved: imminent freedom. As dawn broke, I was up and packed before anybody had even stirred. The walk back down to reception was particularly triumphant, and it was hard to keep from smiling all the way. Wearing my own clothes again felt strange; they smelt a little fusty having been stored in a cardboard box.

I was dropped off at a railway station where I joined the morning commuters heading for work. The first cigarette made me feel sick, but nothing could dampen my spirits. While never wanting to be put back inside, I looked forward to having fun with some of my old friends.

The emotional joy of release soon ran into a brick wall as I arrived at my new home, a big old YMCA. It was like a prison with its long corridors, strangers, little rooms, locked doors, smelly dining hall and plain food. My allocated social worker wasted no time in reminding me that any misbehaviour within six weeks of release would spell an immediate return to detention. Fear of this kept me in line, but an underlying resentment of it started to build.

My mother visited and was happy to accommodate what she thought was my long-held desire to be away from home and free.

18

"How are you doing son? Everything alright?"

"Yeah, I'm fine," I lied.

The truth was that I longed to go home, but couldn't express it. I feared showing any real emotion in case my carefully constructed image fell apart, leaving my identity in tatters. Instead, I waited for the expiry of my six-week release condition to expire, like a cat ready to pounce, then packed-up and left without paying the rent.

Arriving back on familiar territory felt great, and the gang at the precinct listened avidly as I told them about the Detention Centre. Others who'd also been sent to institutions laughed at the memory of their time inside and boasted how easy it had been. I wondered whether they were liars or I was too soft.

Many of the lads stole regularly, making plenty of money week after week, but that wasn't my style. Instead, I returned to drifting around, joining the occasional raid to top up my finances, then disappearing again. My existence was aimless, but it suited me fine. At night I walked the streets, slept on the stairs of tower blocks, or in a shed down by the railway tracks, and sometimes at friends' houses.

I spent many summer evenings alone or with a girl, down by the docks drinking whiskey, smoking and idling around. In winter, I moved into a house where a lot of wild young people hung out. Spray paint covered the inside walls and we steadily snapped up all the internal furniture and burned it in the fireplace to keep warm. The curtains were permanently closed and people arrived all through the night after the clubs were closed to drink, take drugs or boast of robberies and fights.

It was great fun floating around in a bubble of drink and drugs, untouched by the concerns of the world. We lived life pretty fast with everything done for kicks, clubbing, fighting and partying almost every night of the week. Scrapes with the law were customary and twice I escaped a further custodial sentence by the skin of my teeth. However, my air of invincibility came under severe threat in court one day by the police, who tried very hard to have me sent to Risley Remand Centre; a place with a notorious reputation for violence, suicides, misery and filth.

My grandfather, who'd come to offer support, suddenly found the proceedings pivoting around his decision of whether or not to stand bail. As he stood looking uncertain, the Magistrate glanced at her watch and my heart pounded in my chest.

"Come on!" I thought.

"All right, I will," he finally said.

Phew! I smiled with relief while my granddad looked on unhappily. The bail conditions were that I live at his address, sign on at the police station every day and obey a twelve-hour nightly curfew.

Upon leaving the courtroom, I headed straight to the house where I'd been staying to collect a few things and see what was going on. The gang were amazed to see me, feeling certain I'd be remanded in custody. Somebody produced a bottle of Bacardi rum, which I started drinking by the glassful, and as I did, a guy showed up who had grassed on some of my friends to the police.

By including him in the conversation, I gave no clue that I was about to attack, but just as the bottle was nearly drunk, I quickly pounced. He screamed aloud as I beat him with a poker, blood pouring from his head as the others looked on in terror. But suddenly, overcome by so much alcohol on an empty stomach, I collapsed on the floor. Bleeding profusely, the others helped my victim escape through a window and called an ambulance for me.

I woke up the following morning in a hospital bed with alcoholic poisoning, feeling more dead than alive. It's a terrible feeling having a pipe shoved deep down your throat, then watching the contents of your guts pumped out into a glass vacuum cleaner.

The police arrived to escort me back to court, and having advised my granddad to withdraw his bail and save himself a £500 bill, I was sure to be remanded. I stumbled through the court proceedings in a daze before being transported to the place I dreaded – Risley Remand Centre.

> ...looking back at my young self, it
> was clear that i was very different
> on the inside than the outside...my
> true 'self' was becoming horribly
> lost inside the false character i
> was creating on the outside...

CHAPTER 2

Banged Up

The reception area was filled with noise as prisoners were herded through the admission process, all in various stages of undress. Those of us unfamiliar with the procedures clenched our stomachs in fearful anticipation while those who were hardened to it sneered with aggression. Whatever compassion the prison officers may have originally brought to their job had completely run dry, leaving a wall of cold indifference. Nobody cared a damn as we were stripped of clothes, names and dignity as people gazed upon our vulnerability. However, don't misunderstand me; there was no self-pity. I was bad, guilty of many crimes, and figured I deserved everything that was coming my way.

Once bathed and changed we were locked up in a large pen known as 'the cage'. Some of us sat in groups chatting while others perched uncomfortably alone, searching for space in which to stare without catching somebody's unfriendly eye. Later we were taken along corridors to our cells amid slamming doors, jangling keys, shouts and the mingled smell of food and urine. My cellmate, slumped on his bunk, didn't even look up as the door banged behind me.

I presumed mine to be the bottom bunk, there was no pillow and the mattress was filthy and torn. Graffiti covered the walls, the locker was broken and most of the windows were long since gone. The air was constantly filled with shouts between the facing cellblocks, with messages, singing, abuse and threats bouncing off the walls.

Our toilet for most of the day and all of each night was a dirty plastic pot sat in the corner. Most people pissed into a jug and threw it out of the window or crapped into a piece of ripped sheet and flung that out too. On hot days, the stench outside invaded everything and when it rained, a horrifying sludge appeared. Some guys volunteered for the 'shit shoveling party' because after clearing up the mess, they were guaranteed a rare shower, cup of hot coffee and change of clothes.

After being unlocked a few mornings later, two screws rushed past my cell dragging a prisoner along the floor who was covered in blood. I asked his cellmate what had happened.

"He's flipped man, I tell you. He ate his own shit, drank piss, poured water all over himself and sat by the window trying to catch pneumonia."

"What about the blood?" I asked.

"He made me punch him in the nose until it bled, then laid across his bunk with his head hanging over the side, knocking it all night long to keep the blood flowing."

A dark circle of shiny congealed blood lay neatly on the floor like some evil blancmange. Many of the men were living right on the edge, ready to go berserk, break down or commit suicide; you could feel it everywhere.

As we turned away laughing, I realised how little such incidents were affecting me. Everybody's hunger for entertainment was increasingly satisfied at other people's expense or misfortune. It was a dog eat dog world in which we lapped up sick fun like snapping hyenas, giving reign to predatory instincts that chewed away at the conscience.

It was a disgraceful fact that half of the inmates were not convicted of any crime, and a great many of those found guilty would receive noncustodial sentences anyhow. The whole system was a mess that made people worse rather than better.

◆ ◆ ◆

After three months, my case came before the crown court for sentencing, but by then the joy had been knocked out of my life, and I hardly cared what would happen.

Locked in an ancient cell beneath the court building I could almost feel the presence of those who had passed through there before me. Their grief, pain, helplessness and fear lingered with mine.

The courtroom was grand and the judge, all stern pomp. My eyes drifted to the public gallery as my life and charges were tossed about and I noticed a group of students sitting listening to the whispers of their lecturer. In a curious moment, one of the girls turned away and looked me straight in the eye. I envied the peace of her world and she may have envied the abandon of mine.

"Perhaps one day," I thought, "when this nightmare is over, I'll marry a girl just as sweet as you."

Surprisingly, the judge took pity on me and called on the probation service to offer me a work scheme of some sort. However, they refused claiming I'd be too hard to handle. The judge, expressing regret and some reluctance, sentenced me to Borstal Training for between six months and two years.

When I finally got there after spending three months in Stangeways Prison in Manchester, Borstal turned out to be a minefield of petty rules run on similar lines to a military training camp. The physical demands of the regime were impossibly hard and the cell inspections completely unachievable. One tiny crumb at the back of a drawer or a minuscule piece of fluff on the floor meant the cell was unfit for human habitation and had to be totally re-cleaned.

It was less strict than the Detention Center but cleaner and more humane than Remand Center. They offered training in building, welding and catering, along with classes in further education, but I hated the place and refused them all, settling instead for more menial jobs where my thoughts could be my own. "Why should I train for cheap, dirty jobs?" I reasoned. "Life's got to mean more to me than that."

In my heart, I hoped for a life that might hold some significance and meaning rather than the rat-race of a factory or something similar. I could have expected to do just nine months of the sentence, but I had two months added to my time very quickly for absconding. A guy I knew had a friend who picked up a supply of milk early each morning from a small town 15 miles away. We planned to meet up with him, get a lift into Leeds and make a start from there.

We waited until the night-watchman had completed his hourly check, then ran off, climbing the perimeter fence and getting away across surrounding fields. In our haste, running through pitch darkness, we got caught in barbed wire, ripped our clothes in hedges, fell down holes and got covered in cuts and bruises. We kept going for hours until, by daybreak, we arrived at the edge of the town we were looking for.

As we climbed a riverbank to cross the bridge into the high street, police arrived from everywhere and arrested us. This meant more time in the punishment block thinking about what a stupid escapade it'd been.

Life in the 'block' was a completely different world from the rest of the institution. The light was left on 24 hours a day and no furniture was allowed. The books available to read were totally boring and nobody was allowed to speak. I spent most of my time walking up and down humming, whistling and getting more wound up with the terrible slow drag of time. A week in there turned my head inside out.

Back on the wing there was the usual bullying and intimidation, but I took up my customary position of not allowing anybody to push me around. Young men in prison are obsessed with pecking orders in terms of fighting, and debated endlessly over who could beat whom. They allotted me a high standing, which proved beneficial in some ways, but not in others. All too often, a newcomer wanting to prove himself came looking for me; but the whole thing was a false game, we were all phony.

There was a homosexual guy on our wing who was older than most of us. Nobody wanted to appear too friendly with him through fear of being tarred with the same brush. He was playing table-tennis on the table behind the one I was using one evening, and during the game our ball became slightly cracked. Therefore, when theirs came zipping past after a winning shot I caught it and threw ours back without anybody noticing.

After a few shots he walked up, smiling. "Come on, Ricey."

"What?"

"You've nicked our ball. Come on."

"Fuck off. We're playing," I said, and served.

"Oh, come on, Ricey. I know you've switched them."

"Look, you'd better fucking shut it!" I shouted, wanting him to just go away.

We stood there staring at one-another until I threw my bat on the floor. "You two, get out, now," I said.

The other two left, while the guy stood there, bat in hand, shaking.

"Put the bat down," I demanded.

"What for?"

"Just put it down."

After a pause, he pointed the bat in my face and burst out: "Rice, before you start, I want you to know you're an idiot. Why can't you use your brains instead of your fists?"

He stood staring, shaking with sweat.

He was right and I knew it, and I smiled in admiration at his courage while he began looking confused.

"It's this stupid place." I said at last. "Let's just forget it."

He couldn't believe his luck. The bell suddenly sounded for supper, so I offered him a cigarette and we walked to the dining hall together. The lads I'd chased out of the room couldn't understand what was happening. However, my opponent's strength of honesty about his sexuality and courage in standing up against my aggression left me feeling ashamed. He was a better man than me by far, and I knew it.

◆ ◆ ◆

The slow drag of time was torturous and I grew irritated by those who constantly talked about cars, motorbikes and their supposed escapades, most of which were lies. Others turned their cells into shrines to girlfriends, families or heroes. Hostility simmered between people from different parts of the country, but most were actually afraid of each other.

I tried to settle into a routine, not wanting to have any more time added to my sentence. Sport was the one thing that kept me going. We played rugby and football matches every week, interspersed with circuit training.

After eight months, I was given five days home leave in order to prepare for full release, but I had to spend it in a crummy old probation hostel. It felt great to be outside and two of us got the fun started by immediately breaking the terms of our licence and buying plenty of strong lager for the ride home.

The months in Borstal seemed to have taught me nothing as we gleefully drank the booze and smoked cigarettes. Breaking another condition by changing back into my denim clothes, I threw the new suit the Borstal had given me out of the train window as we sped along. I couldn't give a shit. We arrived in Manchester to change trains, but while we were waiting for our connection, a guard approached and asked to see our tickets – unfortunately mine couldn't be found. It was probably in the jacket I'd thrown out of the window.

"We're on our way home from Borstal, mate. We've both got the same parole papers. Look." I said.

He wasn't impressed and didn't like the look of us. "You'd better come with me," he said.

We followed him into a large control room where the local police stood waiting; we were then locked in a cell while they made enquiries. I dreaded to think of the trouble we were in and fully expected to be taken back to the punishment cells in Borstal. After a while, we were taken to the rail chief's office where we stood like two disheveled punks before his large, shiny desk.

"Now, then," he said. "We've contacted your Borstal and they're not very happy about your drinking and loss of ticket. But they want you to continue with your home leave and they'll deal with matters when you return."

I didn't like the sound of that.

"Which one of you is James Rice?"

"That's me," I said.

"We're able to issue you with a… Oh God, no…" he trailed off, looking at my companion with a grimace.

I was confused but followed his gaze and couldn't believe what I saw. My friend was standing there with a smile on his face, pissing himself all over the floor!

"Fuck! What are you doing?" I said, but he just stood there smiling like a lunatic. In a sense, I suppose he was pissing on a world that had pissed all over him. We never saw one-another again after that day, and like many others I used to know, I sometimes wonder how he fared in life.

We were immediately ordered out of the room and back to the police cells; then after being issued with a new ticket and a strong caution for under-age drinking, they let me go.

I completed the journey alone and was met by an irate lady probation officer who'd been kept waiting for hours. She acted like a right bitch and warned me about all the trouble I faced when I got back to Borstal.

"So fucking what?" was about all I could think to say.

After delivering me to the hostel she disappeared as quickly as she could. My life meant nothing to her.

The hostel had a depressing air about it and was occupied by unemployed ex-prisoners who wore grey and beaten looks. After two unhappy days in that miserable place thinking about the trouble that was coming my way, I once again broke the conditions of my licence and ran away to my own area of town to find some of my old mates. Feeling I had nothing more to lose I set about robbing, drinking, fighting and taking drugs with abandon.

The police actively pursued me, but I evaded them time and again. Nevertheless, after a month of living like a madman I began to feel depressed about my life, wishing I'd at least had the stability to manage five days home leave and return like anybody else. The other guys were getting nearer to the end of their sentences, while mine was growing by the minute.

On the streets, my life was a source of intrigue and excitement, but in truth, things were catching up with me. I envied friends who could go home each night and whose futures didn't include the prospect of a life behind bars.

In a desperate search for comfort while out with a girlfriend one night, I asked her to marry me.

"I'm too young and you're too fucking crazy," she replied.

The following day she was furious to learn that I'd asked her friend an hour later!

◆ ◆ ◆

Eventually, the police burst in to arrest me at an apartment where I'd stayed a little too long. Despite the prospect of further sentencing by the courts, I admitted all my crimes, wanting somehow to wipe the slate clean and be free once again.

I was locked up in Walton Jail in Liverpool for a few weeks before being moved to the punishment block at Strangeways Prison in Manchester. After an intensely depressing period in there, I was moved to a secure Borstal and placed on a tough wing. In that place, I was surrounded with a good share of rough characters like myself. Our wing had a bad reputation and the staff hated being allocated to work among us. You could cut the simmering atmosphere with a knife.

A deep hatred began to fester within me as I tried to cope with the long wait for resentencing and an unknown date of release. My cell remained bare and undecorated. "It's not my fucking cell — it's your cell," I'd say to the screws. "Don't expect me to make a home of this fucking dump. My home's outside, not in here."

The screws sent me to the punishment block again and again for all sorts of bad things I did. Those periods were unspeakably painful, but my dark attitude was unremitting and never once did I show the pain I was really suffering.

When I finally attended Crown Court the Judge wanted to add three years to my sentence but relented, giving me Borstal again instead. I'd already served longer than anybody else, but had to start all over again.

My job was coal shovelling, along with seven other difficult prisoners, and we became known as the Banjo Boys. It was the worst job in the Borstal, reserved for the worst offenders, but we couldn't give a shit. In fact, the lower we were treated, the more like animals we enjoyed behaving. Each morning we sat on the coal stack watching the other prisoners file into the big workshops for the day.

I'd been thrown out of my job in the main workshop for running a protection racket. A screw opened my door one morning and announced that the whole Borstal had refused to go to work because of me. Instead, I now filled large trucks with coal, pushed them to the coal stack, emptied them and started again — all day, come rain or shine, over and over. In a sense, I enjoyed the brainlessness of it; shoveling in a daydream.

If one of us reported sick, the screw was obliged to take all of us to the Borstal doctor, which gave us a short break. So, we had a rota for reporting sick.

"Whose turn is it today?" we'd whisper down the line while shoveling.

"I'll have a go," somebody would say.

"Hey, boss, I've got a splitting headache. It's killing me," he would say.

The officer radioed through and we'd all traipse along, a dirty ragged bunch smoking and chatting. No matter what we complained of, the medic gave us two white tablets. Nobody knew what was in them, we just took them. We joked about an imaginary white tablet lorry tipping tons of them onto the floor for the 'white tablet shoveling party' to sort out.

One day, a fat guy called Worsnip said, "Fuck this, Ricey. I'm not shoveling that shit all day in the rain, I'm going sick."

"You can't," I said. "Somebody's already done it."

But before I knew it, he was lying on his back in a dirty black puddle clutching his back, groaning, "Boss, boss, it's me back. I can't move."

The screw didn't look convinced. "For fuck's sake," he groaned, but Worsnip wouldn't let up, almost laughing at times; he came close to getting a good kicking.

A stretcher was called for and we had to carry him all the way while he stifled his laughter. For four days he was kept in sick-bay, being fed and looked after. The next week when he arrived back on the shoveling we all laughed to see him, but he was thoroughly miserable. Being something of a nut job, within minutes of resuming work he was down on the floor again. "Boss, boss, me back, me back."

I couldn't believe it. Surely, he couldn't pull it off twice?

The screw came across. "What's up with you, lad?"

"Me back, boss," he groaned. It was the worst piece of acting I'd ever seen in my life; the smirk upon his lips was unmistakable. This time he failed to keep his own amusement in check and the screw could see that he was messing around.

"Get up, you lazy fat bastard. Stop fucking me about!" roared the screw, dragging him round and round, trying to get him to his feet.

Worsnip was soon back, working alongside us again, having been placed on report.

Meanwhile, I became more depressed, hating everyone and everything. When my probation officer visited, I faced my chair to the window and ignored him until it was time for him to leave.

One day, a lad ran up from behind and butted me in the ear, knocking me across a table. I turned in shock ready to attack him but noticed the screws were standing back.

The guy screamed, "Come on! Come on!"

I knew it was a set up. They wanted me to retaliate in order for me to lose more remission and have me kicked out to another prison.

"What are you standing there for?" I shouted at them. "Do your fucking job and grab him."

Reluctantly they wrestled him down and dragged him away. Later, I was called to the wing's Governor's office, where the other guy stood looking nervous.

"Now what are we going to do about this, Rice?" asked the Governor.

"Well, I don't want you to put him in the block. It's a total waste of time. What does anybody learn down there? I'd rather we just let it go. I'm sick of this fucking place and just want to get out."

After some heated discussion, it was decided that the guy should get away with a warning. "But let me warn you," I said, seething with pure hatred, "put a finger near me again and I'll break both your fucking arms. Understand?"

That incident was the turning point for me. I started keeping myself to myself, living in my own private misery and pain, and as time went by some of the remission I'd previously lost was given back.

Years later I discovered that they'd given up trying to change me and simply let me go free.

My release date eventually drew near and arrangements were made for me to live back at my mother's house; she'd collect me at the gate on the day.

The desire to run mad on the streets had completely gone. Whilst not knowing what to do with my life I certainly didn't want to be locked up anymore.

I always swore that if any screw spoke to me outside the gate after release I'd give him a real mouthful of abuse. However, when the day finally arrived, something inside me seemed to collapse and all I could do was walk in stunned silence toward the car. A screw on his way in to work did in fact shout, "Good luck, Ricey."

But all my fight was gone. "Yeah," I mumbled in reply. "See ya."

My mother had brought some lovely ham rolls and tins of lager for the drive home, like a mini celebration, but I could neither eat nor drink and rode along in a dream. Being out felt worse than being in. I was lost.

◆ ◆ ◆

At home the family greeted me warmly and were supportive in every way they could be. My new Probation Officer, Pat, was a great help, too. One of the few good things that transpired from my time in Borstal was the discovery that I was very good at drawing portraits. I'd joined an art class to get out of my cell one evening a week, but showed little interest in doing any work. However, when I asked the teacher if I could keep a picture of Joanna Lumley from a magazine, he set me a clever challenge.

"If you can draw it, you can keep it," he said.

Over the following week I worked on it in my cell and produced something that was surprisingly good, and was in fact quite beautiful. When I showed the teacher the next week, he was gobsmacked, but I wouldn't listen to him fussing about it and merely took the picture from the magazine I'd wanted in the first place. A few weeks later my cell door was unlocked at an unusual hour and I was told to report to the wing Governor.

"Fuck me, what have I done this time?" I was never out of trouble.

"You drew a picture," said the Governor, "in the art class."

I didn't know what he was on about.

"They want you to put a price on it."

"What! Picture, price...?" I couldn't understand.

"The art teacher put it in a competition and it did very well," he explained. "There are people who are interested in buying it."

I hardly knew what to say and didn't have a clue how to value it, but we came up with a price and it sold very quickly. Spotting an opportunity, Pat, my Probation Officer, found other customers for my sketches and he also got me into his football team. After years of rebellion and being hammered by its consequences, I felt much older than my 19 years. Things were looking good, but would I be able to stay out of trouble?

...it's hard to describe how hopelessly
insecure i felt during those days...
all out at sea...however, some words came
out of me during a conversation with
my mother that revealed a significant
underlying search for meaning...

...sat at the kitchen table thinking of
the mess i was in, i said..."there's a
reason for all this, as if it's meant to
be, like a puzzle I have to work out...
and one day I'll figure it out"...

...the words were spoken in a
daydream, without thought...
but in my heart i knew that if i could
find the key for myself, it would
also be for the good of many...

...at the time of speaking those
words and having those thoughts,
i still faced many tough years...
but when they were over, i did
indeed help a great many people...

...the key to my life became
the key to theirs...

CHAPTER 3

Struggle For Freedom

The price I paid for all my bad behaviour was unrelenting; life had left me way behind and I couldn't envisage how to catch up. My younger sister was fulfilling her potential at college by studying to become a secretary and every day, old school friends drove by in cars they'd bought as a result of having responsible jobs. I couldn't see where my future lay, let alone set any clear objectives. Even when going out for a drink I realised what a great knock my confidence had taken. The pubs were filled with strong young men strutting a self-assurance that was once mine. Compared to them I was a shivering wreck, nervous about all sorts of things, particularly my own violence.

Each fortnight when my unemployment cheque arrived, the money was spent on a night out to a couple of pubs and a club. The drink helped me to relax and mingle, talk to girls and throw off my anxieties. My mother said I should make better use of the money; perhaps buy a watch or some clothes. She was right, but those nights out offered the only freedom from my misery as a has-been failure. My need to be some-body or part of something was strong. The selfish, uncaring attitude I'd displayed for so long in the past was coming back to haunt me.

"I'm a fit young man with good looks," I thought, aching with loneliness. "Surely somebody must want me? Where's happiness? Where's satisfaction?" I'd ask myself.

Employment was hard to come by so I began spending my afternoons sketching or walking. As I arrived home one afternoon, my mother said, "An old friend of yours called here today. Do you remember Denny?"

"Yeah, course I do," I answered.

"Well, he said he would call back tonight."

I was thrilled that somebody was looking me up. None of the old crowd knew where I was living; I kept away from them for fear of getting back in trouble. Denny must have worked hard to track me down.

When he arrived, I was surprised to see how tall he'd grown, the depth of his voice and how mature he was. My memory was of the young-looking kid I'd dumped at the precinct five years before.

We went out for a drink and talked about the things we'd been up to since we last met. Denny had moved south to Sunninghill in Berkshire, where he had a job and a place to live.

"Why don't you come back with me? I'll get you a job easily enough," he said.

I was excited at the prospect and immediately took up his offer.

Within two weeks I'd arrived by coach at my destination but Denny, who was due to meet me, was nowhere to be seen. I phoned a number he'd given me and his sister-in-law came to pick me up. Denny arrived later, looking bedraggled. He'd fallen asleep following a lunchtime drinking session and really, that was typical Denny.

The following day, I met the family in whose house we were to lodge and found them to be lovely people, living in a big house in a well-heeled neighborhood. Within a few days I secured a job as a packer in the dairy produce plant where Denny worked in Bracknell. Keeping busy every day and living in such pleasant surroundings felt really good. The landlady introduced me to cryptic crosswords, which I was surprisingly good at, and we spent many pleasant afternoons trying to solve them.

I worked lots of overtime, which helped me afford new clothes and plenty of nights out; my whole outlook took an upturn during that summer. Future plans including buying a car and taking foreign holidays, became a possibility.

Denny and I had many good times, making people laugh at work or in the local pub. If anything, we took things a little too far, constantly pushing the limits of outrageous behaviour; we had that effect on each other. Having to depend on him for a lift into work each day was a big drawback. It was a 14-mile round trip with no bus service. Waking him up was a nightmare, which often ended in an argument.

We were popular with our workmates and constantly had girls to take out, but the bosses were wary of our slapstick life-styles. One day we clocked on at 6am, having come straight from a nightclub; both of us were drunk and found it hard to stay awake. I got on with a busy job in order to stay alert, but after an hour or two, Denny was found sleeping in a bed he'd made out of cardboard boxes. It was the perfect excuse they needed to split us up and he was immediately sacked off the shift and put on permanent nights.

Without my pushing him, he began taking nights off, and before long my job drifted in the same direction, mostly owing to punctures on my push-bike and bad weather on my commutes to and from work. I got so drunk one night that the police arrested me for sleeping on the pavement. My intention was to keep the incident hidden from my landlady but after being fined in court the following morning, I came outside to find her waiting to give me a lift home. She wasn't bothered at all, but I felt uncomfortable because I'd also fallen behind with the rent.

Denny and I sat up late one night sharing a bottle of whisky while lamenting the backward slide our behaviour had taken after such a good start. We had a lot of fun together but also seemed to be bad for each other. Occasionally we'd return to the lodgings drunk, and while nobody said anything we knew it was wrong.

We opened another bottle and played some Stranglers records while talking. One song we liked was called Don't Bring Harry. To us, Harry was the ugly side of a personality that can emerge through drink and spoil everything. Before going out, one of us would often sing a short chorus as a warning to the other: "Don't bring Harry. I don't need him around."

As often happens when the drink's gone, a craving develops for more. We were in high spirits. "Come on," I said. "I know where we can get some more."

We rode Denny's motorbike to a nearby off-licence intent on breaking the front window, but scrabbling around in the dark for a good rock proved difficult until I had a brainwave.

"I know," I said. "Take me back to the house. I've got just the thing."

We rode back precariously. Then I jumped off, ran inside and re-emerged with a large can of sliced peaches.

"This'll do it," I declared.

"What is it?" asked Denny.

"Never mind. Drive on."

When we arrived, I stepped off the bike and launched the can straight through the window, making a terrible racket. Heads appeared at the upstairs window, but I calmly chose my poison and we sped away. A car driven by a man who'd witnessed the incident gave chase and in shaking him off we were forced to drive on a main road. Before long we were pulled up and arrested by the police. This time we really had gone too far.

After being charged and given bail, I left the area, heading this time into London, but that didn't work out too well, so I decided to try my luck down in Torquay, Devon. At first I made a few contacts in local pubs, but once the money ran out so did the friends. Once again, I felt myself being inextricably drawn back to the troubled streets of my early youth. "At least I'll have some companionship," I thought. Life was lonely.

Arriving back up north and feeling like a failure, I instinctively picked up where I'd left off years before, except this time I was more cynical, violent and moody.

Turning to strong drink and drugs accelerated the downhill process, dragging me further into the pit of disaster. Money for drink and drugs was all I wanted, escaping reality my daily preoccupation. Pretty soon I was arrested for beating up a man outside a nightclub. It was a serious incident which put paid to any hope of going straight. I was slipping off the edge once again. Amazingly, the Magistrates granted me bail, but it proved to be a hopeless mistake as I fell straight back into fighting and trouble.

The police were hunting me down for a whole string of incidents, along with jumping bail and it wasn't long until I was caught. As before, I admitted everything, wanting to be washed clean of all the consequences of my crimes. The depression I experienced in the later stages of Borstal enveloped me immediately as I arrived once again at Risley.

After being moved from one prison to another to face more charges, I was eventually sentenced to two and a half years. Prison life was gloomy and boring, filled with people like myself who hated the system but were incapable of escaping it.

Suicide became a stronger option because any hope of having a decent life had disappeared. My mind and emotions were consumed with hatred. My family tried to keep in touch, but through utter shame I hardly felt able to write back to them.

When eventually the time came for me to be considered for parole, I was looked upon quite favourably. My behaviour had been fairly quiet, subdued mostly. When I was finally granted parole, instead of being joyful at the prospect of an early release, my mind became filled with fear and doubt. The memories of past failures and the accompanying pain came back in a flood.

During a visit from my mother, she congratulated me warmly on receiving parole, but all the same she could feel my uneasiness. I was unhappy and she knew it. A week later she came back.

"I'm not sure about this parole," I said. "It feels all wrong somehow."

"Well, we can work something out once you're free, son," she said, not wanting me to spend any longer in a miserable prison. She'd already commented with concern that I'd lost so much weight and appeared ashen-faced. I was quite depressed, but nobody except her seemed to realise it.

Over the following weeks I was unable to make up my mind about what to do. Despite wanting to refuse the parole, it would be a painful decision that would cause more anxiety to those who cared about me. Therefore, I just let things ride along until release day arrived.

◆ ◆ ◆

It was a cold, dark winter's morning when I stepped out onto the wet busy street and heard the prison door slam behind me. Wanting to blend in, I quickly fell in step with the people headed down the main street toward the train station. Emotionally, I felt rotten, with my hopes only barely kept alive by the letters I'd had from Denny recently. He'd voluntarily gone to prison to pay off some fines but was all set for a new life over in Paris after release. I was interested in going with him but would have to finish my parole period first.

My mother and sister collected me from the station and took me to an apartment I was to rent in the middle of a rough housing estate. It was impossible to see where my future lay; one day at a time was bad enough. I had some money stashed away and began spending it on drink.

One night while drunk, I roamed the streets until the early hours, letting my mind wander all over the place. Staggering home, I bumped into a guy who invited me for a drink. As is often the case with people who sit up late, drinking into the early hours, a dispute arose over nothing and I grabbed him by the throat. Immediately he became hysterical and did everything he could to release his big vicious dog upon me, which was barking like crazy in the kitchen.

Pinning him down while he swung at me wildly, I said, "Look, stop fighting. I'll go and leave you alone, you stupid fucking idiot." But he kept struggling and I couldn't just run because he'd let the dog out into the street to get me.

"I'll have to knock him out," I thought. After hitting him with the underside of a glass bottle, it broke and he slumped. There was blood everywhere and the dog was still going wild. I had to get out quickly. I emptied his pockets, cleaned myself up a bit, then left.

I arrived by taxi in another town, bought a new shirt and got washed up properly. Moving from pub to pub I killed time until the evening before ringing home to see what was happening.

My sister answered. "Jimmy!" she cried. "The police have been here looking for you. What've you done? They're saying terrible things about you."

43

"Looking for me?" I exclaimed. "It must be a mistake. I'll go and see them." My instinct was to calm her fears, but the news she brought meant the end for me.

"Listen, I must go. The money's run out. Don't worry. Everything's all right."

As I rang off, sickness filled my whole being. My life was destroyed and all hope was gone. My plan now was to kill myself. I didn't fancy anything too painful, so I got hold of some powerful pills and a bottle of whisky. Using the remaining money, I'd visit a good restaurant for a slap-up meal, then kill myself in the park. Curiously, having come to that deathly resolve, a peace surrounded me that I hadn't felt since childhood. All the pain, trouble and uncertainty would soon be gone, and I was glad.

Sitting in an Indian restaurant, the food was good, and such was my affable mood that two girls joined me for drinks at my table. Nevertheless, the fun we had served only to remind me of what could never be; it was pointless even trying. Afterwards, I made my way to a quiet corner of a big park and sat swallowing handfuls of pills with swigs of whisky. When it was all gone I lay on a bench feeling dizzy. All I wanted to do was disappear from all the pain, stop hurting everybody else and chalk my life off as a disaster; but soon I felt sick and vomited everything up.

In desperation, I began picking up half-dissolved tablets out of my vomit and eating them again, but it soon became clear that I wasn't about to die at all. If anything, being sick left me feeling better.

"What an idiot! I can't even kill myself," I cursed, feeling like I was being dragged back into a nightmare.

Later, during the early hours of the morning, the police arrested me in the car of a woman I'd contacted. I'd been out of prison for just 10 days.

In the police cells, I sank deeper and deeper into myself, feeling totally unable to cope with what I'd become or the situation itself. The police treated me as though I were a violent psychopath, keeping me under tighter security than I'd ever known. They told me that the man I'd attacked was still in a serious condition and might yet die.

When my mother visited the following morning, I could see in her eyes she was looking at a lost son. There was nothing left for me to say. My life had said it all; it was a deeply tragic moment between us.

On the way to Risley, the police taunted me, rooting for an excuse to beat me up. They handcuffed me to the van bars and threatened to kill me, knowing that with my record for violence, they could blame me for starting it. When we eventually arrived, I was kept in a sweat-box, a tiny cell usually reserved for sex offenders for their own protection. Once out of there, I had to strip off in front of the reception screws before dressing in prison clothing. Instead of putting me into the 'cage' ready for a move on to the regular landings, I was taken through another door into the driving rain. Three screws stood outside with a dog, ready to lead me across a big yard towards the hospital.

"Why are you taking me over there?" I asked.

"Just shut up and keep moving," one of them said, wheeling the dog round and making it bark furiously just inches from my face. "Any lip from you, Rice and you've had it, so move."

As we walked across that dark wet square in the rain, I realised how wildly out of proportion my reputation had grown. To the authorities I was a heartless, unpredictable thug, yet deep down inside I simply felt lost, afraid and desperately lonely.

Once we'd reached the hospital wing, they took me to a strange-looking cell block.

"Clothes off!" barked the screw.

"What?" I asked, incredulous.

45

They backed off a little, again expecting me to punch one of them.

"Just do it," he repeated, drawing a batten from his pocket. "Any trouble from you in here and you'll get a good kicking, followed by the liquid cosh (a tranquilliser injection)."

They handed me a massive pair of nylon shorts and pushed me into the cell and as the door slammed shut, I looked around. It was the worst cell I'd ever been in and helped drag me down to the lowest point of my life. A rough canvas pad was my bed, and the plastic chamber pot overflowed with somebody else's stinking shit. I could see snot and spit up the walls, along with smears of blood. There were no windows, and the light was kept permanently on. I was an animal in a dirty cage.

"Is this my life? Is this all it amounts to?" I asked myself in horror. It was devastating to have desired so much to be free and yet fail so miserably. I curled up on that filthy canvas and cursed the day I'd been born. This time I'd definitely kill myself.

When I was unlocked in the morning, the screws lined the corridor and kept a close watch on me and the other prisoners in this block as we used the toilets and washed. It was my first look at my fellow occupants, and what an assortment they were! Many walked around unshaven and undressed, drugged to the eyeballs. Others wore long shorts and haunted expressions. None of us were allowed any clothes or possessions in case we killed ourselves or somebody else. I learned later that everybody on that wing was in for murder or extreme violence.

After washing, I stole half a tube of toothpaste and a small piece of wood. Once in my cell I stripped the tube down and inserted it into the wood, making a short sharp knife.

"Right, I'll keep this until I can stand no more, then I'll cut my throat," I thought. Suicide was no dramatic step because life was so painful that cutting my throat would be a small thing by comparison.

One day, a little lady in grey visited the cell. She was from the prison church.

"Is your name Rice, James Rice?"

"Yeah, why?"

"I just need to take some details. Now, are you Catholic, Protestant, Jewish or another faith?"

"Is that all you've come to ask?" I answered. "I'm not any religion. I hate fucking religion, so get lost."

She looked ruffled. "Can't you just tell me what you are?"

"No, go away. I'm nothing."

The following day, a priest came to ask if there was anything he could do for me.

"Yeah," I said. "Find out why they're keeping me in this nut-house."

He promised he would, but I never saw him again.

I survived hour by hour, day by day, week by week, until eventually I was taken to court for sentencing.

I knew Denny was inside Risley somewhere, serving time for his fines, and I hoped to get a message to him. Then, one day a work party arrived to unblock our sinks and there he was lending a hand.

"Denny!" I said, punching his arm.

He looked at me in shock. "What are you doing in here? What's happened? I thought you were out."

"I beat a guy up quite badly. I think I'm gonna get a long time for it. I was only out for 10 days."

His face went pale in horror.

I grabbed him by the shirt and said laughingly, "Don't go worrying about me, Denny-boy. I'll be back, no matter how long it takes. Nothing can keep me down. You just get over to Paris and I'll follow you there one fine day."

A screw came to move me on.

"You're unbelievable Jimmy," were Denny's parting words. But back in my cell, I knew it was mostly brave talk. There was no evident way for me to get through this situation alive.

On the day before my 21st birthday I received a four-year sentence for grievous bodily harm and was taken to Walton Jail in Liverpool.

CHAPTER 4

Breaking-point

Four years was better than expected, but it still seemed a crushing amount of time. A glimmer of relief came by way of the two characters I shared a cell with on that first night. One of them, aged about 30, had received eight years for aggravated burglary. He was thoroughly miserable, having left his wife and young children to fend for themselves. It was impossible for him to come to terms with such a big sentence after what started out as a simple burglary.

The other man was a short, stocky gangster, well-known in the Liverpool underworld as an armed robber. He had a 20-year sentence reduced to 15 for a bank job and seemed to be as happy as could be.

"I've only got four left," he enthused. "It's all over for me," he said, rubbing his hands together.

I was only required to complete three-quarters of the sentence, making 32 months in all, which seemed minuscule by comparison. But it wasn't just the time that hurt me, more the complete and utter failure I'd become. No matter how much I detested the system or how hard I tried to clean up my act, the results were always the same. The chains that bound me to that way of life seemed unbreakable. The same situation was played-out in the lives of all the men surrounding me; we were all caught in a web. An air of deadness swirled around the landings whenever we congregated. Each cell housed stories of broken families, abuse, violence, alcoholism, rejection, drug addiction, abandonment, greed, evil, failure and sometimes innocence.

Any fresh optimism brought in by new members of staff was soon choked out of them by the stagnant routine of indifference and mutual hatred. It was them and us; two monsters locking horns in a futile contest, a power game where any notion of rehabilitation was left on the idealistic pages of political spin doctors' portfolios.

After only one night my cellmates and I were split up and moved to share cells with people doing similar length sentences. My new cellmate, Frankie, was doing four years for stealing wagons of meat from the docks. He was a professional who talked very little about his criminal activities.

We got on fairly well and settled down to do our sentence without attracting unwanted attention. Each day we worked in a tailor's shop with a hundred other men, manufacturing prisoners' clothing. My job was to iron piles of shirt collars on an industrial machine before they were attached further down the line. The bored men amused themselves with illegal gambling, drug smuggling, practical jokes and gossip.

After lunch, we were let out to walk around the exercise yard for some fresh air; two circular paths going clockwise were split by another going anticlockwise. The view was of screws standing guard beneath the towering dark walls of the cell blocks all around. We walked in aimless circles, mumbling in hunched-up groups. If it rained we stayed inside, sometimes not getting out for days.

Each morning, afternoon, and evening we were unlocked for 'slop-out'. A whole landing would be let out to place their metal trays outside the door, empty their plastic pots of urine, use the toilet quickly, then get back inside the cell. The slop-out area was small and overcrowded. It always stunk horribly and was degrading enough to spark the occasional frustrated punch-up.

Workouts in the gym offered some relief from the daily grind, but within a few weeks I was banned. My aggressive attitude crept into everything, causing the gym staff to become increasingly worried about the possibility of violence. The last straw came when I removed a steel bar from the dumbbell weights and toted it around as a weapon. This forced me to keep fit by completing a vigorous workout in the confined space by my bed, each night. It was a combination of hundreds of press-ups and sit-ups followed by stretching and a tough ballet routine for my legs.

Being fit was one of the only labels anybody could wear – all other forms of identity had been removed, even our names. Keeping fit, strong and muscular kept up pride and acted in defiance of the stagnating routine that threatened to smoother the life out of us.

Frankie had received an oil-like substance from a friend who smuggled drugs worldwide. It was powerful stuff and could be mixed with ordinary tobacco without detection. I followed my evening work-outs with a cold wash from two big jugs of water, then smoked a long, cool joint before going to sleep.

Meanwhile, Denny had been released from Risley and had indeed made his way to Paris; his irregular letters were a ragged assortment, befitting his approach to life. Although my replies appeared quite casual, they were written with all the craft I could muster, present only in the loneliest of people as I sought to gain attention, any attention. My aim was to somehow reach beyond him into the awareness of anyone who Denny might be in the company of, preferably a female. I presented a frivolous attitude toward my sentence, mocking its small hold upon my unshakeable personality, all spiced with my ability to make him laugh. Perhaps somebody would become intrigued by the source of his mirth. However, the picture I painted was a lie; the sentence was destroying me, and my unhappiness deepened with every day that passed me by.

Some prisoners were prescribed powerful drugs to keep them calm, and I started buying them in a further attempt to neutralise my despair. At first it was cosy to wander around like a zombie for a few days, but after a couple of weeks I began to spiral into deep depression.

Walking around in a state of high tension, my temper kept flaring up for the most trivial of reasons. Sometimes the screws wouldn't unlock me with the other prisoners. Instead, they'd bring me out alone to ensure there was no trouble. Things were getting bad. Being unlocked separately and banned from the gym were signs of the direction my reputation had taken. It made me realise how different I appeared on the outside compared with the reality on the inside: it was like two different people. There seemed to be forces at work within my personality that overpowered all my good intentions.

> ...i remember being acutely aware that
> the person i really was on the inside
> was locked inside a monster of my
> own making; a false personality...

> ...that outer personality was my ego....
> the ego is a false persona created by
> the mind, and it fights for supremacy
> of our life...each time the real me tried
> to simply 'be,' the ego attacked it...

...you may find it disconcerting to believe
that we can build a false personality
that imprisons the 'real' us and
takes over our lives, but it's true...

...as we continue, you will see
how eventually, i had to wage war
against my false personality...
and as a result, i came to experience
being the real me once again...

This state of gloom was lifted one afternoon with the unexpected arrival of a letter from Paris, written by a friend of
Denny's called Genevieve. It seemed a miracle that my scheme
had borne fruit; I was thrilled. The letter itself didn't contain a
great deal, but that was of no consequence. Resisting the urge
to reply immediately, I held back and allowed myself time to
compose a good response, written with all the tact I could
muster. Before long, our correspondence became regular. The
colourful postcards she enclosed bought a flicker of light and
hope to my gloomy world.

It was around this same time that I overheard a conversation in the workshop that caught my attention – and
effectively saved my life. A new guy was telling his friends
about the prison he'd just been transferred from. It had good
food, plenty of sport, and a real effort was made to help the
men sort out their lives through group therapy.

Later, while having a smoke in the toilets, I asked him
about it. "Hey, mate, what's this prison you were talking
about?"

"It's great," he said. "Everybody speaks on first-name
terms, including the screws. It's a therapy place where you
have to sit in groups and talk, but the rest of the time it's easy."

"How do you get there?"

"Just see the doctor. Tell him you're cracking up. They might send you there."

"How come they threw you out?" I asked.

"We got caught making hooch. Four of us got rat-arsed so that was it, curtains!" he laughed. "That's the way it is. If you toe the line its cool, but if you mess with them, boom! You're gone."

A part of me despised him for ruining such a great opportunity; I'd have given anything for such a chance.

"What's the place called, by the way?" I finally asked.

"Grendon," he answered, dropping his cigarette and disappearing back into the workshop.

The idea of trying to get to Grendon started to play upon my mind constantly. Eating good food sounded fantastic, as did sport, fresh air and fair treatment, and while I didn't know much about therapy, I felt sure I could handle it. Despite having become sceptical about my chances in life, something in me lit up at the idea of being helped.

Frankie gave me no chance of pulling off the transfer and called me a dreamer. "It's too much of a long shot," he said.

Nevertheless, I put my name down to see the doctor and took my chances. When I finally saw him, he listened impatiently as I complained that nothing was being done to help me sort out my life.

"I don't want to be in these stupid places all my life. I'm really stuck and can't find a way out," I said.

He offered me medication, but I refused. However, he did put my name forward to see a psychiatrist, and that made me feel like things were moving.

Unfortunately, when the appointment with the psychiatrist came around, I'd forgotten the date and turned up a bit stoned on cannabis. It took all my powers of concentration to engage in the conversation correctly and I hoped to God

I hadn't ruined my chances. After reading my reports and asking a number of innocuous questions, he closed the interview. I returned to the daily routine without knowing how things had really gone.

It was around this time that Frankie convinced me that I ought to stop taking drugs because of the effect they were having, and it took all of my willpower to do so. I almost crawled up the walls such was the terrible ache for more.

A week later they told me that, despite a six-month waiting list for getting into Grendon, I'd be transferred within a few weeks. I was astonished, and Frankie could hardly believe his ears. It was the first time I'd felt excited about anything in a long time. My transfer date soon arrived, and knowing that my new prison would offer a much better life, I left a few of my personal belongings to Frankie.

At a later date, I learned that Walton Jail was as sick of me as I was of it, and they were more than glad to see the back of me. Apparently, I was high up on the list of those expected to either kill or be killed. The psychiatrist was told to get rid of me without bothering with an analysis.

They transferred me in a taxi, and despite being handcuffed to an officer, I loved the drive toward the motorway; just seeing the outside world again was great. The two screws told the driver to pull up outside a pub while they removed my handcuffs for comfort. The prospect of breaking free shot through my mind, but memories of past disasters on the run put me off. Instead, I sat back and made the most of the long journey. It was the first time I'd ever felt relaxed while being taken to an unfamiliar institution.

From the outside, Grendon looked much like any other prison, but once inside, the difference was like night and day.

Gone were the intimidating reception procedures synonymous with entry into most jails. The staff and prisoners were relaxed and easy-going, communicating on first name terms.

After I'd changed my clothes, an officer accompanied me to the induction wing. This was purely because I didn't know the way; normally in Grendon he would have let me go alone. Another officer introduced himself by his first name and showed me to a cell. That kind of reasonable communication was nice but a bit weird.

"Unpack your things, then make your way down to the office if you would, Jimmy," he said, leaving me alone with the door unlocked. Over the years, I'd become used to communicating with screws in a particular way so this friendly approach was very disarming.

While slowly unpacking my few belongings, a warm glow of pleasure filled my heart; everything felt right. When I'd finished I shut the door behind me and made my way to the office, but as I did so the officer came out toward me.

"We don't lock doors during the day, Jimmy," he said. "Too much like hard work," he laughed, turning the lock, and left it ajar. As we walked down the corridor, my stomach tensed up in fear at the prospect of having my things stolen. In prison, you never gave an opportunity for anybody to steal anything. That old fable that there is 'honour among thieves' is a load of garbage. I've seen cons stealing from each other too many times to believe in romantic notions.

I stood by the door while the officer asked questions and filled in forms behind his desk. Each time he lowered his head to write, I arched my back to keep an eye on my cell door along the corridor. There didn't seem to be anybody around but I wasn't taking any chances. Grendon's relaxed atmosphere exposed all my hyped-up fears, making me feel completely out of place.

During that first week, I was placed on an assessment programme of IQ and fitness tests, interviews, initiative exercises and medicals. The staff made it clear that whilst Grendon wasn't a nut house, the main criteria for acceptance was to be of sound mind. I wanted to stay, but behind the scenes there was considerable differences of opinion about whether to keep me or reject me.

"He's too aggressive, too entrenched in his ways, impossible to change, how has he been allowed to come here?" said some.

"He doesn't listen to anybody. His influence on the other men would be far too negative," said others.

However, two senior doctors saved the day. One reported, "He's intelligent, and that intelligence will help him to see that he must change, and then he will." The other, an oddball Australian psychologist who was second in command, said, "This fella told me he listens to John Peel on the radio. That says a lot in my book. I say he stays."

That meeting took place in private, of course. The details of it were only revealed to me a long time after. I never did understand the John Peel factor! They decided to place me back on a young men's wing, which offered more intensive therapy than any other.

There were six groups, each consisting of six or seven lads who met for an hour every weekday morning along with an officer and sometimes a psychologist. In the afternoons, the whole wing gathered in the dining hall to feedback what had happened in their respective groups that morning.

It was quite daunting to talk openly about sensitive issues with the prospect of people chipping in with comments. My initial attitude was to enjoy all that Grendon had to offer, sidestep the therapy and breeze through my sentence. Escaping the deadening drudgery of the big prison system had been an incredible achievement and I was going to make the most of it.

Unlike other establishments where certain prisoners were kept segregated for their own protection, in Grendon we were

57

all lumped together. Rules against violence and intimidation, even verbal, were strictly enforced by an adjudication system upheld by the prisoners themselves. It forced people to be accountable for their behaviour and prevented bullies from meting out their unjustified aggression. It was interesting to see a big shot being challenged by a small person about his abusive attitude or something similar. The big guy often began his defence by picking on his accuser all over again, but soon the group would put the onus back upon him. If he was abusive; it was his own problem and he'd have to deal with it.

People like me who weren't used to being held accountable for our actions found it difficult to keep calm under such pressure and often burst out in aggression. Thankfully, it didn't take too long for the system to soften me, rather than me softening it. Before long, I began to relate to many of the things the other lads shared about themselves in my group. I had a growing respect for their honesty and wondered whether I had the courage to emulate them. It took all of my pluck to raise a hand and offer to do some talking one morning.

"Sure, Jimmy, fire away," they said.

Suddenly, I felt afraid. Was I making a mistake? With arms folded tightly and eyes fixed on the floor, I stumbled the words, "Sometimes when a fight's going to start, I get scared."

There! It was out. That tiny morsel had taken all my courage to say, and in the seconds it took before anyone spoke, I felt small and stupid.

"Do you mean other people's fights or those that you're involved in?" asked the officer.

"Fights I'm involved in," I said. "Sometimes when a person fronts me up for a fight, I get really nervous." I wanted to reveal the truth – that beneath the image I portrayed was a soft, nervous and pleasant young man, but I couldn't go that far.

We discussed it for a while and the other lads helped by admitting to having the same emotions. To them, it may have seemed like I'd hardly scratched the surface of my inner being, but to me it was a giant leap, my first dip into the pool after circling it for weeks. Being honest left me feeling good, even clean, therefore it wasn't long before I identified another item worth discussing and once more raised my hand. A feeling of moving in the right direction began to grow within, bringing a glimmer of hope to my previously dim horizon.

Meanwhile, Genevieve continued to write, telling me more about herself, while I shared with her each step along the therapeutic pathway. I wanted to give some hope to my family but felt all words of promise had been exhausted through a succession of past failures. Actions would speak louder than words. Keeping fit, eating good food and the feeling of achievement did wonders for me. I couldn't imagine having to go back into the Victorian prison system again.

Nevertheless, my willingness to open myself up and challenge others brought its share of problems. After talking through sensitive issues, I was often left feeling vulnerable, especially toward those unwilling to contribute, who sat back looking smug. Pressing-on meant breaking invisible but strong prison house accords, such as bringing people to book for the things they did wrong. A number of them paid lip-service to the regime and kept all the meaningful stuff hidden deep inside. However, the more I rattled the bars of my inner self, the more it created an expectation from the staff for the other guys to do the same.

Some of them began to despise me, viewing my progress as a threat to their defences, but I couldn't stop. Therapy provided the only area of advancement in my life, bringing a sense of achievement I had sorely missed and desperately needed, but the loss of popularity in gaining it was a heavy and unexpected price to pay. Being seen as a traitor to their misguided prison house cause made the journey all the more difficult.

The only thing that made Grendon's therapeutic regime effective were those of us who had the guts to bring bullies and tyrants to book. It was often costly on a personal basis, creating scorn and hatred in others, but without it our little community would have fallen apart.

...i've touched upon this subject many
times during hundreds of talks i've given
to prisoners over the years...
a terrible long-term price lays in
store for those who remain faithful to
largely unwritten prisoner codes...

...before a guy knows it, he's back in
custody, life ruined, opportunities
wasted and utterly alone...

the prison buddies were never
worth the sacrifice...

...in my opinion, the unwillingness
to break such ties and do what's
right is an act of cowardice...

'...the only thing necessary
for the triumph of evil
is that good men and women do nothing...'

...JOHN F. KENNEDY...

Following lunch each afternoon we spilled out onto a big yard to play soccer, during which the lads worked off a lot of steam. Although I enjoyed playing, on many occasions I chose to walk around the perimeter alone, thinking to myself. In the distance, I could see a hill whose slope represented the task I faced in getting well. However, on my imaginary slope, progress was achieved at a high cost. I imagined that in order to gain one foot of ground I had to sink down 19 inches, then come back up 20. The going down represented submerging into the labyrinth of fiery emotions to rummage through festering pain. Coming up meant trying to put my identity back together despite the exposure of fear, doubt, vulnerability and insecurity. The process was exhausting and opposed to my natural instincts of self-preservation.

It came as a wonderful surprise one day to hear from Genevieve that she'd be coming over to visit me fairly soon. From the seed of a letter, sent from the darkness of my desperation, a branch of friendship had developed. The thrill of anticipation kept me going through the weeks before her arrival. Having never seen a photograph, I'd built up a mental picture of her life and looks. I already knew that she was single, 10 years older than me, had a good job, lived in the city and liked to travel. She implied that her visit was primarily to look around London, with me tagged on to the end, but I knew she liked me. On the day of her visit the sun shone beautifully, making her choice of a blue dress seem just right. She, of course, looked a bit different from what I had expected but it was great to finally meet her.

After overcoming the initial difficulties in understanding each other's dialect, we got along just fine. Our friendship, which had grown steadily for a year, was further enhanced by those two hours together. It was great kudos having Genevieve visit all the way from Paris. Just for once, I felt like a real somebody.

Following her visit, I got back to the group work, raring to go. Everything was thrown into the therapy, including one revelation that was the toughest of all. Ever since my time in Detention Center I'd been plagued with occasional homosexual thoughts. The nearest I'd ever come to telling anybody was while drunk with Denny one night years before. Since then I'd carried it around like a dirty secret, feeling increasingly confused and even guilty. It was another example of how little other people knew about the real me. Everything was locked up on the inside and the very thought of telling the group terrified me, but such was my determination to find answers that I came to them one morning ready to spill the beans. The interpretation I placed upon it was that I thought I was bisexual, and that's what I told the group.

There was a stunned silence during which I thought I'd made a terrible mistake; I suddenly wanted the ground to open up and swallow me. The first person to speak was a guy who never said much, but often became angry and swore abuse.

"I really admire you for saying that, Jimmy," he said.

The other lads spoke up too, bringing a good round of conversation and before long, four of them confessed to having felt exactly the same. It was a refreshing meeting during which we were able to laugh at ourselves, say some difficult things and get some perspective. For one of my group mates, being able to open up about the secrets of his sexuality changed him completely. Instead of the aggressive skinhead he had always been, an altogether gentler personality arose, and before he was released, he had a steady boyfriend.

My concerted efforts to find a solution to my life drew the attention of two officers who were religious. I enjoyed chatting to them because they were approachable, but I couldn't understand how they could actually believe in God and enjoy church stuff. Having to sing dreary hymns to a boring organ in a cold, echoing church seemed ridiculous to me. When I was a kid, the priest spoke in Latin, which was even more stupid. One of them pushed his luck one day by giving me a book to read written by an ex-New York gang leader called Nicky Cruz, who'd ended up believing in God.

"You will relate to this man very much, Jimmy," he said, looking triumphant.

> ...it was so strange receiving that book, because as soon as the officer placed it into my hands, i 'knew' I'd write my own; and i did – it's in your hands...

> ...there's a kind of knowing that can fill us with an absolute certainty, but the mind is not able to make sense of it...it's a subject i explore in more detail in my other book, 'Another Kind of Knowing'...

I was irritated by his clumsy attempt to lure me in a religious direction. "Does he think I'm so stupid?" I thought. Therefore, I read the book with a determination to ridicule it. The first half of it about the gangs was good and the story about his conversion to Christianity was interesting, too, but I was never going to admit it.

Strolling into the office one evening, I slapped it down on the desk and said, "The book ends up crap. If this guy's supposed to be so tough, why does he need God? I don't need no God. You get this Nicky Cruz over here and we'll see how tough he is." I spun on my heels and walked back to my cell without waiting for a reply, but in truth, I admired Nicky Cruz for his honesty, but thought Christianity wasn't for me.

After that, I examined various Eastern religions for a while, in the hope of finding the peace I sought. I studied Zen Buddhism and practicing meditation for a while, but failed to grasp the point and grew bored with it. Other beliefs were attractive, but it was difficult to see how they could rid me of my inner 'badness'.

Despite the great effort I'd made since my arrival at Grendon the previous year, nagging old feelings of hatred and violence continued to fester within. Therapy had made no impression on the inner aggression, fear and insecurity that bound me. It seemed that 'Harry' was still around.

At that time, the staff began holding me up as the prime example to emulate. "Look at Jimmy Rice," they'd say. "He's worked hard and he'll make a success of his life, just you wait and see. You could do the same."

Those general assumptions about my future were annoying, although it was easy to see why they were made. I was polite, patient, stood up for standards and was willing to listen to other people's problems. However, frustration began boiling into anger at my inability to root-out the lingering destructive side of my personality. Anxiety about the future returned with the realisation that massive hurdles had to be overcome before being released. Eventually, I decided to bring my concerns to the wing meeting and set the record straight. The staff and lads were seated around the perimeter of the dining hall sipping tea from plastic mugs, wondering what that day's meeting might bring. Some looked nervous, knowing that if they were pulled-up for bad behaviour, the wrath of the whole wing could descend on them. My request to use 15 minutes was granted, and after a short wait I began.

"It's about the way I'm looked upon by everybody. I'm sick of people using me as an example, saying I've got it all worked out, because I haven't. I may walk around being polite and friendly, but the truth is I hate the guts of many of you. If I had half the chance I'd have punched most of you through the wall by now." I glanced around at the surprised faces. "I don't just get annoyed when you do irritating things. I want to knock the hell out of you." I could sense disappointment around the room. "What am I going to do out on the streets after my release when prison rules and regulations are gone? I've acted as nice as pie in here to avoid being thrown out into a big prison again, but that's not how I'm feeling deep down."

I paused, but still no response came.

"Listen," I went on, "the thing is, I don't *want* to hate anyone or hit anyone. It just wells up inside. I can't help it. I want to like people, to be genuine and enjoy life, but I have to wrestle every day with what's inside me."

I turned to a psychologist sitting across the room and asked: "I've tried everything in here. I've torn myself apart, but this hate remains. Where does it come from? Why does it just barge in on my life? Tell me how to get rid of it."

> ...those destructive personality
> traits that 'barged in' on my life were
> the building blocks of my ego...

> ...every horrible thing i'd ever
> agreed to believe about myself
> remained alive within, and held
> me to its destructive opinion...

> ...whatever we come to believe about
> ourselves, governs our behaviour...

All eyes turned to the psychologist as he shifted uncomfortably under the pressure of my enquiry. He talked about 'switching on to happy thoughts' and 'thinking positively' – as if we could shift moods like changing TV channels. As he spoke, people turned away one after another, disappointed in what they heard. We were a room full of men held captive by negative behaviour patterns and nobody seemed to be able to fix them.

"The best way for me to describe my situation," I continued, "is that I'm trapped inside a robot. I've programmed myself to respond to situations in such a calculated way that nobody could ever know what I'm really like. When anything happens, the robot answers too quickly, leaving my true feeling bunged up on the inside."

Nobody knew what to say and I didn't really expect a response. It just felt good to clear the air and be honest.

That wing meeting led to the greatest breakthrough I've ever experienced.

...my description of feeling trapped inside a robot was in fact a perfect interpretation of my ego – not that I knew what an ego was back then...

...over the years, i'd carefully crafted a personality that could be tough, survive prison, never back down, talk smart and act like a crazy man; but it was all completely false...

...the worst thing about creating such a false persona, whether it be good, bad or even religious, is that we become trapped inside of it...who we really are remains hidden on the inside...

CHAPTER 5

Rescued

One person who'd sat listening with keen interest as I vented my frustrations about being trapped inside a robot was Ginny. She was in charge of psychodrama, a form of group interaction that I nicknamed 'the switchblade of therapy' because of its ability to open up people's emotions like a knife. Eight of us were allocated to her class on Tuesday evenings. She was a foxy lady, small, sexy and dynamic. Most of us fancied her but were afraid to say so.

Dramatised role-play was the technique Ginny used to expose buried problems. For example, a guy may be asked to describe in detail how conversations, arguments or general communication took place at home between himself and other family members. Ginny would ask how his mother sat, talked and walked, whether the father pointed his finger, raised his voice or folded his arms. Each of us would be selected to play various members of the family and props were arranged to resemble the family home from many years before.

It always appeared like an ill-prepared drama to begin with; none of us could ever imagine how anything significant could take place. However, when 'mother' spoke, 'dad' asked questions, 'sister' reacted, somebody stared, was ignored or shouted at, the prisoner quickly found himself inextricably drawn into a time, place and situation long since passed.

Ginny watched like a hawk, weighing every breath, noting every word, prompting us with lines and reactions designed to expose the guy's buried emotions. Suddenly he'd be struggling in confusion and Ginny would pounce, like a bird of prey.

"What do you want to say?" she would ask.

"I don't know," he would answer, trembling like the child he had once been.

"What did you do at the time?"

"I hid upstairs and cried. I was angry and hated them."

"What would you like to have said?" she urged.

"I wish I'd told them how unfair everything was. Nobody cared about me," he says, close to tears.

It's extremely difficult for the guy because half of him has become the shivering wreck of a little boy, and on the other is a hard-nosed criminal with a reputation to uphold. A tremendous willingness to do whatever it takes has to be employed by each member of the psychodrama group.

"All right, let's go back through it again and give you the opportunity to say what you really wanted to say instead of burying all that anger and hatred."

We begin once more, again finding it difficult to believe anything significant could come from this role play. Ginny primes 'mother' with a few extras to throw in, to help the process. The conversation soon rattles along and bites deep once again. The guy is pulled to a depth where his emotions can't stand much more. He pauses, lip quivering, finely balanced between pulling out and an emotional collapse, and Ginny's on the edge of her seat.

Finally, he explodes with all the tears and words he's carried around for years. It's so deeply personal that the rest of us feel awkward and fall into the background. While we quietly roll cigarettes, Ginny's there like a mid-wife, cradling his crying head. "Keep talking," she says softly. "Tell us what's happening inside."

We've witnessed a child, a boy all broken to pieces. Moments later over coffee the guy talks about what he's seen or realised, while Ginny tries to package the thing back together. The value of re-visiting past emotional trauma cannot be underestimated, but time is short; the lad will be alone in his cell within half an hour and needs to come to terms with what's taken place. Ginny's philosophy appears to be one of undoing knots in the past to bring freedom in the present.

She turned straight to me as we got settled into our seats for our usual Tuesday session.

"Jimmy, why don't you use the group tonight to tell us more about the robot you described at the wing meeting?"

I couldn't imagine how talking about it could make any difference, but agreed to participate anyhow. After describing in more detail what I'd meant, Ginny asked, "Would it be fair to describe your robot as a wall, Jimmy?"

"Yes, I suppose it would."

"Okay, why don't you go and sit in the corner while we build a wall around you with these chairs? Then you can tell us more about it."

When they'd finished, she asked me to tell the group why the wall was there in the first place. I sat thinking about this for a while without knowing exactly what to say.

"To be honest," I said, "this wall's here to protect me. It protects me from being hurt physically and mentally, too."

Ginny then asked me to tell them when and why I began building the wall. That was more difficult to answer. I couldn't remember a particular time when my behaviour had stopped being genuine. However, I did remember something that had happened on the school bus when I was seven or eight years old.

"I was just an ordinary kid like anyone else," I said, "messing about with my friends during the ride home. Then suddenly I was punched to the ground. My nose was bleeding and I struggled back to my feet in sheer panic, trying to stave off the attack. He was bigger than me, but to my surprise, I got the better of him. Then much to my relief, the bus conductor came and dragged us apart. He shouted at us, stopped the bus and threw me off. Although I was afraid of violence, and didn't want to have a fight, the incident transported me from being a little nobody into a little somebody. I'd been involved in a real fight and had blood all over my face. I'd also beaten a tough-nut and been slung off the bus."

That incident certainly wasn't the root of all my evil, but the advantages I'd taken of it were typical of how I'd constructed my false personality over many years. Exploiting the benefits of a perceived reputation had proved to be as addictive and hard to resist as any drug; once created, it possessed me.

After hearing my story, Ginny arranged us like the inside of a bus and cleverly selected a guy to play the attacker whom I didn't see eye-to-eye with anyway. We ran through the incident again and again. Every time he attacked I refused to fight and stayed on the floor, doing my best to behave in a way that was truer to my real self. My attacker taunted me more and more and I could see that although he was only supposed to be play-acting, there was a gleam of satisfaction in his eye at seeing me humbled in this way. Ginny had set it up very provocatively, and by the fourth time through, I was exhausted and feeling quite vulnerable. The guys were beginning to see a real, softer me, that I'd kept hidden for years. Sensing an opportunity, Ginny urged the other 'actors' to slip out of their roles and call my reputation into question.

As they did so, the cost of pressing on became more and more difficult. If I were to dismantle the tough robot I'd become trapped inside of, it would leave my 'true self' horribly exposed.

When eventually she thought we'd done enough, Ginny told me to return behind my wall of chairs, but as I made as if to rise to my feet, she played the killer card: "No, don't stand, you must crawl."

Her words impaled me like a spear. Every last part of me screamed against doing this, knowing I was about to inflict irreparable damage to my false personality. If I crawled across that room, my reputation would be in tatters and there could be no going back. But, as I leant upon my knee, stuck in the agonised decision about whether to do as she had asked, a deep and quiet courage arose from within,

"I must do this," I thought. "I must do anything to break this reputation, this false image, even if it means humiliation. I want to be real; I want to be me."

As I began to crawl, prompted by Ginny, the bully stood over me and mocked, "We can all see it now, eh? You're nothing. I can kill you any fucking time I like."

I never thought I'd make it to the chairs; it was the hardest thing I'd ever done in my life, like crawling across broken glass. When I finally sat behind the wall, something emotional stirred deep down inside that had been missing since I was a boy. Suddenly, I felt like I'd rediscovered that simple lad I'd been in the first place, an ordinary young man, almost boring, and in a way, I loved him. As the group talked all around me, I couldn't hear a thing.

"Where do I go now?" I wondered. "Nothing will be the same after this."

Before being locked up for the night, we talked about the session and I thanked the group for their help. It had been so traumatic for me that I felt sick and confused. Later, in my cell, I felt deeply sad at never having been the person I truly was. In reality, the crawl across the floor had broken my ego, enabling my true life to arise from within, but at the time, I had little concept of such psychological issues. I could have done with having somebody to talk to – my emotions had been ripped apart and it was hard to get my bearings. The saddest part of the whole thing was seeing who I might have been if things hadn't gone so horribly wrong. Underneath, I'd always been a decent person, but I'd never given him a chance.

...it took a number of years for me to realise the enormous significance of that night...my ego had been blocking my 'true self' from experiencing life, but once it was broken i came to find new life...

...when we break with the ego, it allows true 'life' to arise...there is a reservoir of it in every person...crawling across that floor was how i broke out of my ego, but it had been up to me to take the step...

...everything that followed, as you will read, was the inevitable outcome of the actions i'd taken...

All prisons have at least one character, and Grendon's most memorable was Ernie, the night watchman. He came on duty at 9pm when all the officers were going home and the prisoners had been locked up for the night. He didn't have any keys to open cells, but had to turn a night clock at the end of each landing, which recorded his hourly tour of the cells.

Night watchmen usually ghost around unknown and unseen, but not Ernie. He had a good word for every lad before the lights went off at 10 o'clock. His simple countryside accent made him a warm grandfatherly-type figure to most of the lads, many of whom shared their news with him each week. He could be heard laughing, making his way around, talking through the cracks in the doors and striking matches to keep his pipe lit.

He and I got on fine but there were occasions when, feeling a bit low, I'd pretend to be asleep and let him pass by. After my rigorous psychodrama and general feelings of insecurity, I once again let him pass me by and lay in the dark listening to his conversation with the lad next door.

Feeling stuck for something to say, the lad asked, "Hey Ernie, do you believe in God?"

"Oh yes," he said in his country drawl. "I read me Bible every night and say me prayers, giving thanks to God for all I've got."

"You would!' I thought. Another brainwashed church-goer was all we needed to hear. For the life of me, I couldn't understand how anybody could seriously get involved in church and religion, but I was in for a surprise.

Their conversation soon trailed off and, after brief chats with the remaining lads, Ernie disappeared. To my surprise his words about thanking God kept rolling across my mind and it occurred to me that I wasn't grateful for anything. Despite making a terrible mess of my young life there was much to be thankful for, but all I ever seemed to do was feel sorry for myself. 'Life' had been a free gift to me, but who was I supposed to thank for it? I had talent, ability and potential, but where had it all come from?

"There must be something or someone who made me," I thought, wandering up and down my cell. As I stared at the door, hands stuffed inside my pockets and bare feet on the cold floor, I decided to give thanks to the 'thing' somewhere out there in space that had made me.

"Okay, Jimmy-lad," I said to myself, "let's give thanks to the *thing*." It seemed right, but to speak audible words seemed ridiculous. I struggled to know what to do.

"Come on, say it," I urged myself.

Suddenly a light turned on in my head.

"Hey, this is who God is. This is the God that everybody talks about."

All I wanted to do was say thanks – no church or religion – but once again, I found it really difficult.

"Give God his due, Jimmy," I said to myself.

My head shook in disbelief. What the hell was I doing? This time I really was going crazy. My face flushed with embarrassment even though nobody was there, then with my eyes looking all around, I stood awkwardly and muttered, "Thanks, God."

Once it was out, I loosened up a little and continued. "Yeah, thanks, God, for my life and my health and my fitness and everything you gave me."

Although I'd smashed the gift of a healthy young life through riotous living, it seemed right to be grateful for being given it in the first place. After doing so, I felt curiously clean and refreshed, then slept better than I'd done for weeks.

The officers continued to claim that I'd done very well and would be sure to make a success of my life, but I wasn't convinced. The ship of my life was heading toward those treacherous waters of release, upon whose rocks my life had been battered again and again. Nightmarish scenarios, fears and uncertainties filled my mind: "Have I done enough? Can I ever break free from the stranglehold my badness has upon me, or will I have to commit suicide as planned from the beginning?"

As floods of concern filled my mind, I suddenly had a vision of a mountain similar to the one I'd often seen from the exercise yard. From top to bottom I could see thousands of my imperfections, all of them obstructing the freedom I so longed for. I turned away with my heart sinking as another vision rose up out of the floor. This time I saw a large black porthole in which I stood naked, cradling filth that dripped down my body. No sooner had the vision disappeared up into the ceiling than another arose out of the ground. The horror of the things I held to my breast disgusted me.

Then suddenly, instead of those things rising up, everything accelerated and it felt like I was falling into the blackness from where the visions had come; and then, the boy at the heart of me cried out, "God, please help me!"

Almost before the words were off my lips, the terrifying fall stopped and I floated as if suspended by a parachute. The horror was gone, replaced by a massive sense of relief. As I stood there, shaken from the whole experience, great tears welled up inside. I couldn't hold them back.

As I fell to my knees, pictures of all my past hurts and pain flooded through my mind and I cried every tear I'd never cried. It was as if, while gritting my teeth through the living hell of life on the streets and prisons, a dam of sorrows had built up inside me. Now the dam had broken and everything was coming out.

Along with those memories came others of my wrongdoings, savage fights, theft and destruction – the whole thing was awful. Through agonised tears I cried, "Oh God, I'm so sorry, I'm so sorry." I remained in that state for a long time until eventually, saturated in sweat and tears, I curled up on my bed and slept in peace.

In the morning when the doors were unlocked I woke with a sense of freshness I'd rarely felt before. Politeness to the other lads rolled off my tongue with genuine ease, rather than the usual grudging effort. Little did I realise the kind of dimension my life had entered into. I wondered how long the good mood would last, but by lunchtime I was still breezing along when I bumped into Gerry, one of the religious officers.

"Hi Jimmy," he said in his usual friendly manner.

"Hi, Gerry," I replied, feeling glad to see him. "Listen,

Gerry, I want to be a Christian. What do I do? Where do I go?"

He was completely taken aback and stood in shock for a moment before responding.

"What's bought this on, Jimmy?"

I hardly knew and didn't even know why I'd spoken such words. I quickly rattled off the story of what had happened in the cell the night before and he almost choked on his pipe.

"Do you have any books I could read?" I asked.

"Yes, Jimmy. Get your lunch and I'll show you them later."

As I took my place in the lunch queue, my mind went back 11 years to an incident in secondary school one afternoon. Every student in my year assembled in the main hall for a special presentation. I was quite excited until I realised they were handing out Gideon New Testaments. What a stupid waste it seemed! As I walked out through the gates at the end of the school day with a few friends, I turned to them, Bible in hand, and said, "What do they want to go giving us these things for? What good are they?"

The others murmured in agreement.

"I'm throwing mine away," I said. "What do I want it for?" I then started ripping pages out and let them flutter onto the ground. The more I ripped out, the more uncomfortable my friends became. Sensing their concern, I turned up the heat. "Come on," I said, "why don't you rip yours up, too? You don't believe in God any more than I do."

More pages fell to the ground.

"Come on," I pressed. "If you believe in God, keep your Bibles. But if you don't, throw them away. What's the use of keeping them if you don't believe?"

Nobody said a word, each of them held motionless by the challenge. Worried looks crossed their faces and I wasn't surprised. I half-expected the great fist of God to appear from the sky and knock my lights out. Tossing the book into the gutter was the signal for us to move along, and typical of 11-year olds, we were soon talking about other things.

Whilst eating lunch I felt sorry for what I'd done to that little book all those years before. In my mind, I threw up a quick message to heaven.

"Hey, I'm sorry about what I did. But if you give me another one, I'll take care of it this time."

After lunch, Gerry took me to a small tea-room where a large collection of books filled one wall. There were all kinds of important looking titles to read, but I knew exactly what I was looking for. My eyes skimmed the shelves quickly. "Come on," I thought.

Then suddenly, hidden among bigger volumes, I spotted a little Gideon New Testament and snatched it up in glee.

"Can I have this one?" I asked, holding it up.

"Yes," replied Gerry, showing me another book. "You can have this one too and…"

"No, no," I cut him off. "I only want this. Can I keep it? Can it be mine?"

"Yes."

He didn't know why I wanted that book in particular, but he simply granted my wish.

That evening I could hardly wait until lock-up in order to begin reading, and once I got started I couldn't stop. Occasionally, I put the book down and considered what had taken place over the past few days of my life. It was amazing. I'd smashed the robot that encased me, discovered who I really was deep down inside, called out to God, felt transformed, cried my heart out, told somebody I wanted to be a Christian and was now reading the Bible. Was this really me?

During the weeks that followed I spent less time watching TV or playing pool in the evenings, preferring instead to sit alone in my cell reading my little book. The lads would stop by to ask why, but I hardly knew how to answer – I just felt such peace.

Before long, they started to congregate in my cell, sitting all along the bed and around the floor while I told them stories from my little book. None of it was intentional, but just happened. We were like a bunch of kids.

I began to realise that the hope I'd been searching for had arrived. With a certainty that is beyond description I *knew* that everything had changed and I'd never be going back to prison again. My life had been rescued and a fresh start had begun. I'd spent years pacing up and down prison cells with the gut-wrenching frustration of never having fulfilled my potential, but now, things were going to be different and I knew it with utter certainty. My purpose in life would be realised, my role fulfilled. It was exciting to be given another chance.

As my new hope grew, other more vain ideas regarding the future fell away, the first of which was the need to live in Paris. Going there suddenly seemed pointless – I'd already found what I was searching for. Why would I seek my hope over there when it was already in the palm of my hands?

...over the years, i've often wondered about my immediate decision to become a christian...what direction would i have taken if i'd been indian, jordanian or perhaps japanese?...

...it's clear to me that there is a realm beyond, a stream of 'life' that each world religion claims to be its own; but it is in fact neutral and belongs to all people and no single group...

Having applied for parole once again, I was fortunate to have my old friend, Pat Halpen, as my Parole Officer. We hadn't been in touch for a while so I sent him an honest account of what had happened to me.

We'd first met when Pat was given the dubious pleasure of being my Probation Officer while I was in Borstal at the age of 17. I'd hated probation people and lost no time in telling him to go and fuck himself. However, I soon learned that he could give as good as he got, and I suppose that's what made me like him.

After seeing me incarcerated once again following Borstal, and then failing after only 10 days on parole, he could be excused for doubting my ability to make it in life. Pat knew my potential, but feared I'd been locked up for so long, had so many fights and set-backs that I was beyond redemption.

My letter contained more than the collection of empty promises prisoners so desperately want to believe about themselves. At a later date, he shared with me quite unashamedly that the letter had reduced him to tears. And with Pat, I'm not talking about an 'arty-farty' sort of guy: he was an ex-bus driving, Irish-blooded Evertonian; a 6'2" centre-half who'd never shied out of a tackle in his life. Something of the magnitude of my change had jumped off the pages and hit him. Jimmy Rice was free!

When Denny heard that for me the old ways were finished, he wrote back with unusual swiftness, asking for a visiting order so that he could come over from France to see me. His reaction was totally out of character; for him this world held nothing of sufficient importance to raise more than a smirk.

I dispatched the visiting order and looked forward to seeing him again. On the day of the visit he turned up two hours late, with only 30 minutes remaining of visiting time. I'd spent the afternoon playing pool, wondering whether he was ever going to arrive. The staff allowed us some extra minutes together in view of his long journey. He looked tired, had lost weight and was bedraggled after hitch-hiking the entire way.

Denny earned his crust from busking around the Champs-Élysées in Paris. It was a hard life but offered excitement, freedom and, occasionally, very lucrative earnings. He hated the winters and swore each year that he couldn't face another, but many seasons were to pass before he finally sought new pastures.

It's the custom for the visitor to bring cigarettes, but this time I had to borrow one from an officer for Denny. We greeted each other warmly then sat back looking at one another with a smile. I couldn't help but notice the difference between us: I was in great physical shape, bright-eyed and smiling, while Denny seemed drawn, tardy and unhappy.

We exchanged small talk over a cup of tea before he leaned forward in a more serious tone and asked, "What's the score then, Jimmy? What's been going on around here?" His smirk suggested he hoped whatever had happened to me might not be real.

"I don't know, really, Denny," I said, forgetting what I'd prepared myself to say. "I just feel different now and I can't go back to my old life. Its finished mate."

Looking across while blowing smoke through his teeth, Denny realised that my change ran deep. This was more than mere words. He'd come to Grendon doubting the possibility of my life being so radically altered, but now he could see for himself, and his fears were becoming true. You can't kid your friends.

Our friendship was old enough to deal with the silence that followed before he continued in a more serious tone.

"Look Jimmy, I've known you since we were kids, and I always thought you were a nutter, the genuine article. As we got older, you frightened me half to death with the things you got up to. But I'm not like you. I was just pretending, hanging on to your shirt-tails trying to keep up." His eyes grew glassy and his voice sank deeper with meaning. "But now you've gone home and I'm stuck out here alone. I don't know how to get back Jim…" He trailed off, his voice betraying the emotion of the boy I'd known so many years before.

His instinctive understanding about the gulf that now separated us woke me up to its reality. He was lost and I was found; he was dead and I was alive; he was lonely and I'd come home. Denny knew I had always been honest about my badness, and never wanted to pull the wool over anybody's eyes. If I'd been trying to kid him he would have spotted it in one moment. That's why he visited me, to see with his own eyes.

Therefore, we sat in the knowledge that our friendship would never quite be the same again. I had departed from that which bound us together. We embraced before parting and as he turned to leave I saw a sad character whose direction was lost. Despite returning to the playground of Europe for a life that many would envy for its abandon, in the light of my freedom he was the one in chains, not me. Denny may never have glimpsed the darkness of his situation nor I the brightness of my own had we not sat face to face in the visiting room that day.

A week later, I received the astounding news that I'd been granted parole once again and would be released within weeks. It was highly unusual for anybody who'd broken parole by committing violent crimes to ever be granted it again. However, it became the first of a great many doors that opened as if by magic throughout the rest of my life. Something inside me 'knew' that the past was gone and the future had come.

Being granted parole meant I entered into a period of prison life that is without rival. Having served almost three-and-a-half years, with only a 10-day break on parole, those final weeks were spent in an increasing sense of peaceful euphoria. I'd finally triumphed over the agony of arrest, charges, remand, sentencing and prison itself. But more importantly, I'd overcome Jimmy Rice. The memory of past release dates remained bitter, but I was no longer afraid. On this occasion, thanks to breaking my ego and coming into the realm of heaven's bright lights, I felt elevated above every possible concern. The sunshine had come out inside of me and it was like starting my life all over again.

A Christian lady called Annette urged me to make contact with a church when I got out, stressing the importance of meeting with believers. I'd visited the prison chapel a couple of times but they seemed to have formalised the life out of something that was supposed to be uplifting.

Although I couldn't quite get my head around the connection claimed by Christianity, between the cross of Christ and the change that had happened to me, something truly extraordinary had indeed taken place.

Before I left reception on the final day, an old lifer shook my hand and wished me well. "Good luck, Ricey. You'll do alright son. I've got a lot of admiration for you. Don't forget to have a drink for me."

"No, I won't forget. Thanks. See ya!"

For me, leaving Grendon was almost sad. I'd been through so many dramatic experiences in there, but eventually I'd received more than I could ever have dreamt of.

On the train home, I fell into conversation with a delightful young lady from Bournemouth. She was travelling up north for an interview at a university. After asking the reason for my journey, she was fascinated to learn that I was on my way home from prison. This led to a whole variety of questions, the answers to which amazed her more and more. As the train sped along carrying lives to an assortment of destinations, a true story of unusual content was unfolding before her eyes. The prison gates had closed the chapter of a tempestuous life that had been rescued at the eleventh hour.

The train was pulling me along into an exciting future of boundless possibilities. What a far cry from past times when I'd be staring out of the window deep in thought, smoking cigarettes and sipping lager from yet another can. The very memory of those nightmare days sent a shudder down my spine and I thanked God it was all over.

...it would be fair of you to ask how
i could simply 'know' that it was all
over...after all, people throughout the
world are held captive to all manner
of destructive behaviour and cannot
simply walk away...they may hate
what they are held to...detest their own
behaviour...but still, they are held by it...

...my 'knowing' was far superior to
any desire or regret...more powerful
than mere belief...when i broke the ego,
i was released from that which had
imprisoned me...and i was truly free...

...being able to see our ego identity
is very difficult...because it's
who we think we are...

...35 years have passed since i walked
out through the gates of grendon prison,
and not one thing i came to 'know' about
my future has failed to come true...

CHAPTER 6

A Daily Choice

I arrived home in a much calmer and settled state than on any previous occasion. It was July, the sun shone brightly and the days were long and hot. I didn't want to rush off looking for work immediately, but needed time and space to make the adjustment to outside life. It may surprise you to know that release from prison, despite being so deeply desired, is extremely hard to deal with. Fortunately, being so deeply assured about my future, I was free of such fears.

On most days over those first few weeks, I packed a lunch and set off for West Kirby, a lovely coastal town on the west tip of the Wirral. At low tide, I walked out across the massive expanse of sand to sunbathe behind one of the three islands off Hilbre Point. Sitting there looking out to sea in the beautiful sunshine was a wonderful experience; the warmth seemed to soothe my very bones. I wrote letters of encouragement to friends left behind in Grendon, along with others to Genevieve and Denny in Paris.

After a while, I attempted to start up a window cleaning round but failed to win enough customers. After resurrecting my drawing ability, I gained a number of commissions for portraits, but the income proved too slow and the work over-intense. As the world woke up each morning and began to operate like a big machine, everybody had their part to play. It was frustrating for me standing on the touchline without a role to play; the need to be involved in something meaningful grew into an ache.

Annette continued to write, encouraging me to join a church, stressing the importance of meeting with other Christians. I wanted to do this, but the thought of walking into a place full of strangers was quite daunting. I kept putting it off. There was no urgency in me, because I 'knew' what I 'knew' – that my future was assured. Attending church would not make the promise any more certain.

Reading my little Gideon New Testament wasn't as easy as it had been in Grendon either as there seemed to be so many distractions. Living back with my family and staying out of trouble may appear to be a success in and of itself, but I needed my own space in which to 'be' the new man I had become. It wasn't as simple as reverting back to the person I'd been before all my troubles began, because in many ways the younger Jimmy had ceased to be, and I'd become a completely different man. I'd become somebody my family had never really known, and I had to 'pretend' to fit in.

With the job market so unfruitful I turned my attention to further education and professional qualifications as it made sense to me to invest some time in creating a future for myself. Pat found me a small class whose aim was to help adults brush up on Maths and English, or otherwise prepare for exams of some kind. After visiting the lecturer, completing a couple of tests and finding the place friendly, I signed-up for the next term.

It was with utter joy that I got out of bed and prepared myself for class on that first Monday morning. Having somewhere to go, a task to fulfill and a part to play was a huge relief. Riding along on the bus with school kids, workers and others who had busy days ahead, made me feel I'd joined the human race. I made a good start and enjoyed the challenge, but my progress was interrupted after only one week by Pat, who phoned to ask whether I'd like to take part in an outdoor activity course that was starting the following day. It was hard to know what to do, but my teacher helped by suggesting it was an opportunity not to be missed, so I accepted.

The next day, Pat took me to the Operation Drake Fellowship Centre (now Fairbridge) in Conway Street in Birkenhead. Their objective, as a result of the riots in the early 1980s, was to re-motivate young unemployed people from the inner cities through adventurous outdoor activities. The staff greeted me warmly and explained that the course would last for 10 days, the first five engaged in local activities and the remainder camping in the Lake District.

After filling in a form, I was asked to wait in the large kitchen area where others also sat around. As we hadn't been introduced to each other or given something to do, an awkward silence ensued. I was reminded of the many uncomfortable situations I'd experienced when entering prison reception areas. Having waited in such discomfort for over half an hour, I decided to clear off home; I'd much rather be studying in college.

The following morning, I phoned to ask whether anything would be happening, and after assuring me that things were now in full swing, I made a return. There were 12 of us in the group, 10 male and two female, along with three instructors. We sped around Merseyside from one activity to another, stuffed into the back of an undersized minibus. We tried rock climbing, abseiling, shooting, canoeing, orienteering and some team games.

Much of it was fun, but a running feud soon developed between the staff and some scallywags in the group who locked horns early on and remained that way until the end.

Those young tearaways made me laugh with their street credibility and dirty looks. But I feared for their futures, knowing full well what some of them were heading toward.

Rain accompanied us on the long drive to the Lake District and drizzled upon us for three consecutive days as we trekked over the hills. One lad threw his bag down and ran off during the first climb. His friends said he'd either steal a car or hitch hike back to Liverpool. But the only thing he broke into was our minibus, where we found him two days later looking cold and miserable.

As trouble continued to flare between staff and lads, I found myself walking the middle ground, defusing situations after having gained the respect of both parties.

On our return to Birkenhead we unpacked the kit, had a cup of tea and were then presented with a smart certificate proving we'd completed the course. These were to be used at job interviews to demonstrate that, despite being unemployed, we had been active. Although I was grateful for this experience, I couldn't help but notice a lack of 'people skills' among the three staff members. All too often they remained aloof from the group and missed opportunities to bond with us. In my opinion, their lack of sensitivity was the cause of the 'us and them' mentality that spoiled things somewhat.

Nevertheless, despite the course being fraught with difficulties and littered with flash points, it felt like a real achievement to have completed it. Such was my sense of gratitude to this maverick organisation who'd reached out so freely to help me, that I ran a sponsored half-marathon some time later and donated the money to them.

They offered follow-up courses on sailing ships, along with conservation projects in Scotland, and made us welcome to visit the Centre at any time. I declined the offer of any further activity, however, and refocused my attention on my education. Little did I realise that the pieces of the jigsaw of the next nine years of my life were falling into place.

◆ ◆ ◆

Back in class, I passed two City & Guilds exams in Maths with distinction, and was then encouraged to sign up for Maths, English and Sociology 'O' levels at Birkenhead Technical College. In order to keep pace with the work, I attended an evening class twice per week where a teacher helped with the subjects I struggled with. His name was Mr Bromilow, and I'll never forget the patient kindness he showed me.

As the workload increased, so did the desire to leave home for a place of my own. There were no problems, but something inside me had changed so much that I felt out of place living among my own family. In fact, I had to get used to being a whole new me. Whatever I may have been in the past was gone forever.

Pat put me in touch with a housing association called Stonham who provided accommodation for people like myself who, having messed-up in life, were looking for a fresh start. Following an interview, they agreed to offer me a room, but unfortunately, they had nothing to offer in the area I pre-ferred, so I had to wait.

"We've got a lovely place in Birkenhead, though," they said. "It's just been renovated, overlooking the park. Why don't you try that?"

"No thanks, I'll wait."

Meanwhile Annette kept bugging me to attend a local church, but I couldn't be bothered. Nevertheless, I woke up with a bit of a hangover one Sunday morning and ran off to the nearest church service. It was a big Anglican place where the people were quite friendly, but there was a coldness about the whole set-up.

The following week I visited a less formal fellowship where things were so free and easy that people kept standing up at odd moments to shout out, read the Bible or sing. Sometimes they were all doing this at the same time and I couldn't make head nor tail of it. Three women were baptised by being completely dunked in a tank of water. Their testimonies were very emotional, with many family members and congregation crying.

I failed to appreciate that 'life' itself was carrying me along very nicely of its own accord, and began to feel a bit guilty about not joining a church. Added to this was the frustration of waiting for the right vacancy to arise at Stonham. Each time I phoned them, they continued to suggest I try the house in Birkenhead. Eventually, out of sheer exasperation, I agreed to look at the property just to shut them up. When I arrived, I found it to be a big house that had been completely refurbished. Four of us would share the place, each having their own large private room, while the kitchen, bathroom, shower and living-room were communal.

I took a key and ran upstairs to look at one of the vacant rooms, and as I sat on the bed, peace immediately flooded through me.

"I'll find my way again in this room," I heard myself say. My mind was immediately made up to stay. Something deep inside told me I'd found the right place.

Within a couple of weeks, I moved in and started the next chapter of my life. My room had a nice view overlooking Birkenhead Park, which I used for my running and cycling. It was an ideal location, being just walking distance from college, the Drake Fellowship Centre and shops.

The first person I got to know was a guy called Robbie, who had a wife and family, but through a succession of disasters had ended up living alone. During a long conversation, I told him how my life had been completely changed by some kind of spiritual experience while serving a prison sentence. Robbie told me he'd had a hit-and-miss relationship with God for many years on account of alcohol, but now wanted to sort it out. He also told me his brother-in-law was the part-time pastor of a small chapel in the middle of the housing estate behind our street. He suggested we try it together, so I agreed to give it a go one Sunday.

Having my own space allowed me to listen to my own music, collect some interesting books and live life on my own terms. The new 'life' I'd found in Grendon had been somewhat dulled during the six months living at my mother's house, but now it began to glow again. Sometimes I'd step back from myself and wonder what sort of man I was becoming. The music I listened to was Mozart, Tchaikovsky, Bach, Strauss and Handel; none of which I'd grown up with. Along with that, my book collection consisted of many Russian classics such as *The Idiot*, and *The Brothers Karamazov* by Dostoyevsky, *Oblomov* by Goncharov, and *A Day in the Life of Ivan Denisovich* by Aleksandr Sozhenitsyn.

I visited art galleries, museums and public gardens, read all the most fascinating science magazines and started learning about local history. In a curious way, I could no longer relate to the people I'd grown up with and much preferred my own company.

During that period, I felt it high time I went to visit Denny and Genevieve in Paris. I was a little embarrassed at never having visited a foreign country and wanted to get on with it. The message that I received in Grendon about 'having everything restored' was strong within me, but first of all, I needed to get myself a passport.

After putting off visiting the chapel with Robbie for a few weeks, I finally agreed to go. It was a square-shaped, flat-roofed building of modern design surrounded by flats on one side and a busy fire station on the other. The congregation consisted of a handful of old ladies plus a few odd bods scattered about.

We were greeted warmly, though I would have preferred to remain anonymous. Never had I felt so uncomfortably out of place than sitting there dressed in my combat jacket and jeans – they were the best clothes I had.

I couldn't remember a word of the service, such was the discomfort of trying to make it through and at the end my escape was blocked by old ladies at the door who wanted to shake my hand and wish me well. What a relief to hit the pavement and breathe fresh air! I felt exhausted.

During the following week, the pastor, Peter McGrath, visited me and we had a good laugh. He was an ex-docker who'd been locked-up in Borstal himself as a lad. He now worked for the Seamen's Mission among the dockers, sailors and prostitutes along the many miles of Merseyside's busy waterfront. He was a down-to–earth character who'd been transformed into one of the nicest men you could ever wish to meet.

It was the warmth of Peter and his wife, Sheila, along with the genuine care of the others that drew me to visit the church again the following week. There was something very real about those people that cut across the age and culture gap between us.

In Peter, I found a good example I could model myself on over the coming years. His personality contained the graciousness, love and kindness that I admired. He tailored his sermons to suit my limited understanding, spoon-feeding my hunger for knowledge week by week.

After a few months, the old ladies kindly asked whether I might like to try a bigger nearby church with more young people in case I became bored.

"To be honest," I answered, thinking back to my prison days, "I've had enough of young people. I just want to understand what Christianity is all about."

I accepted that there were no shortcuts on the road to working out my life's journey; the world owed me nothing and I'd have to figure it out.

Unemployment was very high in the area where I lived and the police were almost overwhelmed trying to deal with a major heroin epidemic. On a number of occasions, the windows of the church were smashed by gangs of marauding kids, as we met to pray. Along with that, we regularly arrived to find the church had been burgled, and visitors often had their cars vandalised.

Fortunately, I'd got to know members of the local gang whilst on the course with Drake Fellowship. Having been to prison a few times for violence made me acceptable in their eyes, which came in handy when bumping into a nasty crowd hanging around a street corner late at night.

"Alright Jimmy," I'd hear from the darkness.

"Alright lads," I'd say, and stop for a quick chat.

During that dark winter, two ships sailed into the docks that brightened our lives considerably over two memorable weeks. The Logos and Doulos were crewed by hundreds of young Christian people from all over the world, belonging to an organisation called Operation Mobilisation. The ships called at ports all over the globe, where the crew ventured out into the local communities to spread the good news about their faith. Many of their stories were like my own: rescued from prisons, drug addiction, prostitution, slavery or war. I visited the ships after college each night to enjoy their fabulous meetings.

During their stay, an appeal was made for young believers to join the ship for a two-year stint and I wasted no time in collecting the application forms. It was the best offer I'd heard of in years.

On my frequent visits, I became friendly with Mario, a young man of my own age from Guatemala in Central America. He'd come to faith after being put in jail for drug offences, and what a conversion! He went on to spend his life helping others. Mario brought people from various nations to visit us at our house each evening; we loved their company and the stories they told. A little Peruvian woman in a brightly knitted hat and gloves sat on the edge of the sofa and became completely engrossed watching snooker on our television – which was even more fascinating to us, because she had no idea of the rules and the set was black-and-white!

After 10 days, the application forms for joining the ship remained incomplete on a shelf in my room; an apathy seemed to have set in regarding them. The next time I saw Peter, the Pastor, I mentioned it to him.

"Hey, Peter. I'd love to sail on one of those ships. I've got the application forms but I couldn't be bothered filling them in. I don't know what's up with me."

After a pause, he asked in his genial way: "Do you think God may be telling you to stay, Jimmy?"

The idea annoyed me immediately! I didn't want God interfering with my plans. Being stopped from anything was always sure to get my back up, yet beneath my reaction there was no denying that something inside me was reluctant, in a big way.

"I'm not trying to tell you what to do Jimmy, but you need to consider whether it's the right direction for you."

For certain, travelling the world would give me something to show-off about and stick two fingers up to a prison system that had failed to destroy my desire to live. The other motive was to live my spiritual life wrapped within the cocoon of that loving organisation and be shielded from the reality down on the street.

The final day of the ship's visit arrived quickly and, before I knew it, Mario and I had embraced for the last time to say farewell. That night as I lay in bed thinking, I remembered how sad Mario had become one day when I played some classical piano music on my hi-fi system. He said it reminded him of his sister back in Guatemala.

"Why didn't I give him the tapes?" I thought to myself. "Get up and do it now, you lazy bugger." Outside the house strong winds drove rain in sheets across the freezing town. I didn't fancy the idea.

"Come on," I said to myself, pulling back my cozy bed-clothes. "Let's do it."

Slates were being blown from house roofs as I ran along the wet pavements to the docks. The ship lifted up and down in the storm, but looked unguarded, so I clambered up the steps and sneaked on board to search for Mario's cabin. After finding it, I pushed the door open but was halted by his room-mate, a Dutchman, who shushed me quiet.

"What do you want?" he whispered. "Don't wake Mario. He has to be awake very early."

I told him about the tapes and left them on his little table. It would have been nice to hand them to him in person, but to do it in secret would be a nice surprise, and I went home feeling good.

The following day it was back to the grindstone, working hard in class. I had lots of homework to get through that night, so after supper, I sat watching the news by the fire, preparing myself to start. Suddenly there was a knock at the door and Robbie went to answer it.

He shouted through: "There's a surprise here for you, Jimmy."

I thought he was joking and kept my eye on the TV, but when I looked up, there was Mario standing in the doorway.

"It's too windy to sail," he said smiling. "We'll try again tomorrow."

What a joy to see him again! As usual, he'd brought a companion with him, this time, a gentleman called David

Fox, an old man from Ohio who looked almost round in his big sheepskin coat. He asked about my life and when I told him the story he was moved to tears. David left me his address, and we struck up a friendship that I found supportive through a number of tricky years.

It was sad for Robbie and I to see those ships sail away; they had been such an inspirational breath of fresh air for both of us.

"Wouldn't it be great to sail away with them for a couple of years?" Robbie said later over a cup of tea. "We could go to the meetings, get all that help, then come back here and have it all worked out."

I knew what he meant. The journey of life was not easy, especially being so young in our faith, we were constantly tripping up like kids learning to walk. We both enjoyed the occasional night on the beer, smoking, and a flutter on the horses each Saturday.

"I don't think it's like that, Robbie," I said in reply. "If you're willing to learn, God will teach you everything you need to know right here, *within these streets.*" As the words left my mouth, I knew I had said something emphatically true for myself. A voice immediately seemed to speak within my head: "And that's how it'll be for you, Jimmy. If you want, you can learn it all within these streets."

In that moment, heaven was revealing the challenge of a plan for my life over the coming years. The college of my personal training would be the streets of Birkenhead. In one sense it was a thrill, the kind of crazy struggle people were apt to sign up for, but in another I was disappointed. It seemed like my dreams of travelling the world, chasing the sun, completing a degree were suddenly under threat. However, reality told me this was the way it had to be. Every building needs a foundation.

There was no use kidding myself: I was a rough diamond that needed cutting into shape. Robbie wondered why

I suddenly left the room but such was the weight of the real-isation unfolding before me that I needed to walk around the park and think it through.

"Has it been real?" I asked myself. "Can heaven really speak to me through my own mouth?"

As the months leading up to my college exams passed by, I gave the message less thought and waited for things to develop, hoping that God would somehow change his mind.

...it's very interesting for me to read this chapter again and see my younger self struggling to understand the extraordinary transformation that changed my life...

...however, those efforts led me into the error of thinking that i could grasp the vastness of eternal life with my mind......but the human mind is in fact diametrically opposed to the heavenly realm...

...enlightenment cannot be experienced with the mind...

...the mind is only interested in creating
an earth-bound personality, which we
may call the ego...such an ego may even
be constructed of religious material...
but that doesn't make it spiritual...

...no matter the make-up, even if its
religious, the ego brings nothing but
judgement, intolerance and misery...

CHAPTER 7

Rocky Road To Love

During that time, I kept up my visits to the staff and young people at the Drake Fellowship Centre. Some courses included young people from Derbyshire who were recruited from a youth café in Chesterfield called The Wall. One day, as I sat on a table in the office, a girl appeared near the door who looked out of place. Remembering the discomfort of my own first day, I tried to make conversation by asking whether she was on the present course and where she came from. However, her single-syllable answers suggested she wasn't interested in making conversation, so I gave it a miss, but somehow, she stayed in my mind.

Meanwhile, my proposed trip to Paris was made all the more possible by the purchase of a 10-year passport. I'd never had one before and felt excited about using it, but deep inside me there was trouble. The idea that I should remain 'within these streets' only seemed to fuel my desire to get away. Everybody else seemed to be travelling here and there, so why shouldn't I?

First and foremost, I had my college exams to think about. I felt satisfied that no matter what the results turned out to be, I'd worked hard and revised well. In the event, I managed a top grade in English and reasonable results in math's and sociology. A whole year had elapsed since my release from prison and I felt good about the way things had gone. The weather was warming up again, a long summer break was in store and I'd kept myself in good physical shape.

At the Drake Centre, I was invited to take a place on a bridge-building project up in the Scottish Highlands. I wasn't terribly keen until a name on the list caught my eye; Joanne Riley from Derbyshire. I felt sure it was the same girl who'd snubbed me some months before; therefore, out of a roguish curiosity, I agreed to go.

Thinking of her reminded me how much I missed having a girlfriend – I was often quite lonely. The few liaisons I'd experienced since release had all been short-term and disappointing. I wanted something more meaningful and lasting; I'd even started praying to God to find me a wife.

The object of the course up in the Highlands would be to build a bridge across a small river that would enable the foresters to avoid a massive detour during the winter when the river was in flood. On the day we were due to travel up to Scotland to start the course, 12 of us turned up in dribs and drabs carrying an assortment of bags, cameras and cassette players. The Drake Centre looked like a bomb had hit it as we moved kit from the stores onto the trailer.

Joanne Riley was indeed the girl I'd spoken to previously, and thankfully, on this occasion she was much more relaxed and willing to talk. She was the only girl on the course, therefore as soon as we hit the road, a contest for her attention began in earnest. I kept myself in the background, not wanting to make my attraction toward her so blatantly obvious.

The long journey, though scenic, grew increasingly boring as darkness fell, but eventually, after ten and a half hours we pulled into a tiny forestry village called Taynuilt in the Highlands of Argyle.

Desmond, the ranger, greeted us and invited the whole crew into the living room of his warm cottage. He soon had us making stacks of toast, sipping a 'wee dram' of whisky and guzzling mugs of tea. His springer spaniel slept in front of an open log fire, and as our eyes glistened in light of the flickering flames, we wondered what manner of man he was to live without a TV?

Desmond was a bright-eyed, straight-talking man who took a personal interest in everybody, explained things thoroughly and expected us to work as hard as he did. At around midnight we moved to the large shed where we were to camp in and tried to get some sleep. However, the midges had other ideas and began biting my poor English legs and kept me up half of the night scratching.

In the morning, we split into groups to start a variety of tasks: cutting wood, shovelling stones for cement, rust-proofing girders, digging banks and preparing meals. The rain drizzled on us for days, making conditions difficult and extremely muddy, but everybody worked hard, regardless. In the evenings, we swam in the lochs, played Shinty (wild Scottish hockey) and had fun shooting Desmond's shotgun. I liked to make Joanne laugh when we were together and began enjoying her company more each day.

At one stage, Desmond asked Joanne and I to make a large wooden box that would be filled with cement to form one of the pillars upon which the bridge would stand. I deliberately let her make the box the wrong shape in order to spend more time with her correcting it. Desmond couldn't understand how we had made such an elementary mistake!

After working flat-out for five days we were given a well-earned break in Oban, a harbour town surrounded with islands. Everybody woke up early and set to washing, shaving, brushing hair and trying to look smart in the creased clothing we pulled from our bags. Arriving in Oban, we made a beeline for the nearest pub and within minutes, the juke box was playing, pints were being pulled, cigarettes lit and balls lined up on the pool table. I noticed Joanne didn't seem to be enjoying herself and I wanted to ask her to go out for a walk, but I felt nervous of being rejected. Instead, I took a gamble by rising to my feet and saying within earshot, "Blow this for a lark. I'm off for a walk." As I took the first step toward the door, I hoped upon hope that she'd come with me.

"Can I walk along with you?" came the magic words. I couldn't believe my luck.

"Yeah, come on," I said casually, trying to stay cool.

The only problem now might be if somebody else wanted to come with us. I'd timed my move to coincide with them all having a full pint they wouldn't want to part with, along with the pure joy of the pub atmosphere – and I was right.

Suddenly, we were out on the pavement submerging into the busy streets of the lively tourist town, where we wandered around talking about everything. The best part was spent overlooking the beautiful bay from McCaig's Tower, situated high above the town. It was up there that I began to fall for this Joanne Riley, and so began the painful turmoil of love. The time spent alone with her did nothing to satisfy my desire to be with her, but enflamed it into a permanent ache.

Over the next couple of days, I treasured every moment of her company, making her laugh, helping her out and trying to act cool about the whole thing. She had to leave for home two days before the end of the course, and for the sake of my rattled emotions I was glad to see her go. It would be easier with her completely out of sight. I'd never felt that way before – pain mixed with joy, happiness with sadness, brightness with raging darkness. I didn't like being tossed upon the seas of such high emotion and did all I could to rein them in. Nevertheless, there was no disguising my delight when Joanne suggested we exchange addresses and keep in touch. But what was I thinking? She had a steady boyfriend who had money, and she lived miles away in Derbyshire. In reality, she'd soon forget somebody like me.

As for the west coast of Scotland, it was by far the most beautiful place I'd ever seen. I couldn't believe that such an incredible landscape existed at the far end of the same British soil that I'd grown up on; it was so completely different.

As the course drew to a close with the successful completion of the bridge, we returned to Merseyside and dispersed to our respective homes.

...the emotion i felt was like
being thrown around by a wild
horse... i had no control...

...it made me realise why one
of my favourite poets, charles
bukowski, wrote the infamous
line...'love is a dog from hell'...

No sooner had I arrived back at the house than the prospect of visiting Paris arose again. I avoided discussing the issue with Peter, the pastor, for fear he might talk me out of it. I was having a difficult time with the Christian life because it seemed to be so restrictive and caused me to second-guess myself at every turn.

The real problem was that I believed the Christian God had been involved in saving my life and was protecting me as I walked along the way. Therefore, I didn't want to fall out with 'him' in case he let go and my life tumbled back down the hole it had been rescued from. A guilty conscience grew within me that nagged, "How can you act badly after all that God has done for you?" The whole thing was a pain in the ass.

Nobody can live that way and be content. It was an unhappy alliance that persisted for a number of years until eventually I broke free, but in the meantime, I soldiered on.

The fact that I'd already told people that I was going to Paris made it harder to turn back; my pride wouldn't allow it. I didn't want to be all talk and no action. Therefore, while shopping one afternoon I pushed all doubts to the back of my mind and bought a return ticket. I wasn't used to having to pay attention to an inner voice, and it annoyed me having to wrestle with it so vigorously. I'd be glad to go and be done with it.

After travelling to London by early-morning coach, I caught another to Dover along with a group of holidaymakers and took the hovercraft to Calais. After exchanging some money and passing through Customs I continued by rail across country to my destination. Genevieve had agreed to meet me in a small café near the Gare de Lyon.

After finding the location quite easily, I ordered coffee, rang Genevieve's office and sat waiting. An hour later we were together and it seemed so strange. The first time I'd written to her I was deep in the depths of despair; a prisoner without hope, and now we were standing on a Parisian street looking at one-another. She seemed quite distracted, as if I'd arrived at an awkward moment, but once we'd eaten a good meal, the atmosphere relaxed.

I'd avoided alcohol for a few months, but when Genevieve ordered a bottle of champagne I allowed myself the indulgence. In letting it pass my lips I was deliberately weakening my resolve and shoving that nuisance of a conscience out of my holiday.

Each night we ventured out onto the busy streets, visiting bars and theatres, playing pinball, eating meals with friends and having fun. I knew Genevieve had fallen for me but she held herself back, wrestling with something unseen. During the days while she worked, I travelled on the metro all over the city, visiting the sights, jogging around the parks and meeting up with Denny.

Seeing him again wasn't the fun I'd expected it to be – perhaps seeing me was a reminder to him that I'd sorted my life out and his was something of a mess? During our conversations, I couldn't help but notice that his life was fairly aimless, not much use to himself nor anybody else. My mind flashed back to the time in Risley when I bumped into him whilst on remand. It was hard to believe I could have rescued my life from such utter despair.

In an effort to meet him half-way and relive something of the past, I spent an afternoon drinking with him in an Arabic bar near the Arc de Triomphe. We had a good laugh beating all-comers on the pinball machine, but the owners weren't too happy about us clocking-up so many free games. Unfortunately, as the afternoon wore on Denny became increasingly abusive to those around us, acting a little more outrageously with every drink that passed his lips. It was a rough establishment where violence could erupt at any moment and I had to keep a close eye on things. However, Denny was at his belligerent best, turning his back on the Arab owner to play another game after telling him to fuck off.

At the point where things were about to get out of hand I managed to persuade the locals to hold back while simultaneously dragging Denny out of the door. It was a horrible reminder of a life I could never return to, pushing our luck to the limits and living on the edge every day of the week. It came as no surprise to learn just a few months later that Denny had been stabbed in the street.

That night, we stayed at his apartment across the city and as he slept, I sat looking out at the Parisian skyline knowing that something was finished between us; it was time to go home. Something morbid inside him was constantly drawn to stare death and danger in the face. It's the way it had always been. As for me I'd been neither the reformed character nor the wild man of old, but had fallen hopelessly into a grey area between the two. I'd stood for nothing and acted like a hypocrite to both worlds; an experience that was wholly unsatisfying.

The last couple of days spent with Genevieve did not go too smoothly either. Similar to Denny, she was pleased that I'd found a new life, but also knew it would draw me away from her. She was mostly annoyed at allowing herself to fall in love with me. At the train station before departure, I stood next to her feeling like an empty fool. Instead of speaking openly about what was really going on, I'd glossed over it and acted like everything was alright.

As my train pulled in, I said, "Goodbye, Gen. I'd better go." I leaned forward to kiss her cheek but she pulled back.

"Jimmy, just go home to your God," she said.

I stood there feeling dumb.

"Just go!" she repeated.

I walked to my gate feeling hurt and embarrassed – it was the end for us, an unhappy conclusion. The leanness that had sat heavily upon my soul from the outset of that excursion became a dull ache and weighed heavily on me all the way home. Upon my return, in an effort to clean up my conscience (which was in fact an over active mind) I attended all the chapel services, even punishing myself in an act of penitence by joining the most boring of them, but no matter how hard I tried, guilt clung to me like a leech.

On one particular afternoon, I'd had enough of it. In frustration, and tired of being pushed down, I began spitting out angry words while poking the air with an accusing finger.

"Devil! I know you're here. I'm sick of you trying to push me down. I hate you. You've tried to ruin my life right from the start. You loved it when my family were brokenhearted because of my imprisonment. You laugh when people destroy themselves with the things you tempt them with.

"Well, I'm getting back on my feet. I'm a fighter who'll never stay down. No matter how many times you knock me down I'll get back up. There will never be a day when you can forget about me. I'll keep trying to win people over from your evil clutches.

"You're trying to pile the guilt on me so I'll be ineffective, but it won't work because I know that I'm loved – I'm set free. It's a fact that you can't change, that's why you have to lie. So get out! Go!"

As I finished talking, the heaviness lifted completely and a lightness returned that I hadn't felt for weeks.

...in reality, the 'devil' was in fact my own egoic mind condemning me...as soon as my 'real inner self' arose and overruled the mind, true eternal 'life' was able to flow from within, as you will see...

Just as I was ending my rant, an inner impression said: "Go to the office." It wasn't audible, neither a feeling nor a thought, but a clear message. I didn't know how seriously to take it but decided to ride up to Pat's office in Laird Street anyway. Unfortunately, when I got there they told me he'd gone out. Therefore, just to cover the bases I made my way back down to Conway Street and visited the Drake Centre instead. As usual the big office was busy with phones ringing, everybody talking and people coming and going. I sat near the door minding my own business, but when I looked at the boss, Dougie, I noticed he was staring at me with a curious expression.

"John, is Judy still on the payroll?" he asked the bookkeeper, keeping his eye on me. While John checked his paperwork Dougie rose to his feet and kept up his strange stare.

"No, she's finished now, Doug," John finally said.

By then I was beginning to feel a little uncomfortable under his gaze and thought perhaps I should leave, but suddenly he spoke to me.

"Do you want a job, son?"

I was shocked. People turned to listen.

"Well, yes. Is it a proper job?" I asked.

"Yes," he said, standing behind his desk.

"Not a temporary government scheme?"

"Nope."

"A proper instructor's job?"

"Yup."

"Wow! Thanks, Dougie." I couldn't believe my ears! "When will it start?"

"Today, son. You're working for me right now. You can spend the afternoon helping out."

Suddenly, I felt claustrophobic; it was all a bit much. I wanted to be an instructor but not this afternoon. I needed space to run and shout and breathe.

"But I've got to do some things this afternoon," I lied. I didn't expect to be working all of a sudden, and it caught me on the hop.

"What things have you got to do?" he asked bluntly.

"Well… Er, just things, Doug. You know…" I was struggling; the need to get out burned within.

"Okay," he said after a pause. "Let's have you in here at nine in the morning."

"All right, thanks," I said. "See you tomorrow."

I left without looking like I was in a hurry, but once outside I bombed around the streets on my bike with my head in a whirl.

That evening I phoned my family, members of the chapel

and some friends to let them know the good news. When I
was asked my level of pay, working hours and conditions of
employment, I didn't know a thing!

...in my mind i couldn't quite work
out what had happened...what or
who was the devil?...how was i able
to behave contrary to my own faith,
then simply shove the guilt away and
receive such a great reward?...

...the reality took years to fathom...
but just as i'd become trapped inside a
violent egoic identity in prison, (one that
I called a robot and broke free from)...

...once i joined myself to a religious
faith, my mind started to construct
a whole new ego image...and despite
it being religious, it was equally as
troublesome and tied me up in knots...

...i'm not saying religious faith
is false, but a personal identity
constructed by the mind, even if it
consists of a religion, is false...

...why are such religious egoic self-images
so troublesome?...
...because they turn against the believer
with condemnation and wrongly judge

those whose beliefs differ from their
own...there is no love within the ego...

...after returning from paris my own
ego tried to condemn me...but my 'true
inner self' rose up against it...(the ego
is no match for the true inner self)...

...the moment the ego was rebuked and
shoved aside, the true force of life that
we are connected to had its opportunity
to flourish and open the way for me...
as you will see from my story, this
dynamic happened many times...

The day had been eventful. Before going to bed I remembered the confrontation with the devil (whoever that was) and the voice that followed, instructing me to 'go to the office'. It was incredible to think that heaven would actively speak to me and move on my behalf.

Back into my mind came the unpopular message spoken after the ships had left: that I could grow 'within these streets'. The new job was a piece in a jigsaw that was fitting together; the power of 'pure life' seemed very close. My experiences were working against the odds. I was an ex-convict with a bad record, little work experience, few educational qualifications, living in an unemployment blackspot, but was given a great job in a depressed part of a depressed town.

That job was to be the launch-pad from which my potential would be drawn out and developed, a job in which I'd face up to some hard facts about life. It was also one in which I'd become a man.

...from the very beginning of
my transformation i have been
regularly gripped by a 'knowing'
that arises from within...

...however, that 'knowing' was only
ever able to flow when my egoic
identity was exposed and rejected...

...as mentioned previously, my ego
tried to construct my personality
out of religious bricks, and they are
the hardest to reject, because it can
feel like we are rejecting the very
heavenly realm that loves us...

...that's precisely why jesus gave the
religious people of his day such a hard
time...they may have strictly followed
the decrees of their faith, but it was
all carried out in their minds, causing
them to be cold and prideful...

...it's not difficult to identify a religious
ego...it will always place more importance
upon the sanctity of its beliefs than the
followers themselves...it will preach
love, but believe it has the right to kill
and condemn...it will be intolerant of
other faiths and beliefs...it will always
be rooted in fear and insecurity...

111

...more than anything, it will make constant use of the words 'believe,' and 'belief'...an ego has to 'believe' because, being a derivative of the mind, it cannot under any circumstances 'know' the truth...

CHAPTER 8

Joanne

Shortly after finding my new job, I decided to move out of the house with Robbie and the other lads and began sharing a friend's apartment nearby. Mark was part Afro-Caribbean, loved his reggae music, wore a permanent smile and stayed up each night making disco speakers from old cupboards and drawers. The flat was situated in a rough area with no shortage of incidents, but I spent most of my time away on the job and saw little of it.

As for the lovely house I left, I was sad to hear that it fell into disarray within months of my departure. Internal doors had been kicked in, things stolen, bathrooms flooded, strangers came and went and all trust between the residents vanished. Finally, it had to be closed down for a long period of time.

The first two courses at work both incorporated trips to the Lake District, working with difficult groups in glorious summer conditions. My team leader was Arthur, a nutcase ex-paratrooper who sometimes needed to be controlled as much as the scallywags! Once I'd worked alongside him on a canoe expedition however, we got on fine and shared a lot of laughs.

Applying the lessons I'd learned from my first experience of Drake courses, I set about making it as easy and friendly as possible for the young people when they first arrived. I knew full well that no matter how tough they might appear, there would always be apprehension about coming into an unfamiliar situation among strangers. After putting the group at ease and explaining what the course would consist of, we spent five days moving from one activity to another all around the city. The idea was to awaken them to facilities available in their community that they could take part in afterwards. Also, step by step, we taught them all the skills needed for the five days we'd spend in mountains of the Lake District. They learned rudimentary map reading, how to secure a climbing harness, tie knots, abseil, basic canoeing, sailing and as many other games and activities we could cram in.

Slowly and surely the group would form into a working unit and start to govern itself; and that's what we were always looking for – leaders to arise from within. At night, while camping by a fire, they were reminded of how good life can be without drink and drugs; the countryside was there for everybody. It was great to see different group members feel themselves becoming revived and express their desire for a better life. That's precisely why we were based within the city – to help maintain the flame of hope we had revived and offer further projects for them to join in once they were home.

It was fantastic being paid to help those young people through the medium of such amazing outdoor activities. Walking, resting, climbing, eating and camping with people for just a few days created a tremendous bond. It was a wonderful experience in which genuine trust and growth could be achieved.

Over the years, I went through the full extreme of highs, lows and everything in-between regarding these young people's lives. For example, I remember one December afternoon being invited by a young fellow called Gary to visit his new flat. He was so proud to be getting on his feet and wanted to thank us for our encouragement. Soon after we helped him gain a place on Operation Raleigh where he conducted three months' conservation work in Kenya. Nobody would have ever thought that possible when we first met him.

Nevertheless, during that same week I was handed a message to, 'Call Billy when you can'. Such notes were regularly left on my desk. Billy was a strong young man with tons of potential, but had spoiled a number of opportunities through drug misuse. However, he completed a few courses with us and things seemed to be turning around; he had such natural ability that we had it in mind to make him part of our team. It was almost Christmas when I wrote a reminder to call him in my diary, but such was the busyness of that month, I had to delay doing so until the New Year. However, before Boxing Day arrived he was found dead, and I couldn't believe it. For a long time afterward I'd see his name and phone number in my diary and wonder whether I could have made a difference?

Billy wasn't the only one to die and Gary not the only one to reach such heights – we saw it all. That's why we reminded one another in staff meetings never to link our own performance to the outcomes of the young people's lives. We delivered the best courses possible and encouraged everybody as much as we possibly could, but what they subsequently did with their lives was out of our hands. "If they do brilliantly, don't take too much credit," I'd say, "and if they fail, don't condemn yourself. Just be happy that as a team we did a good professional job." The last thing anybody needed was staff floating too high, then falling into despair.

After a few weeks in the job, I was handed a pay slip for £350. I'd forgotten all about wages and received more than I expected. Kenny, my fellow instructor, had to help me open a bank account to pay the cheque into, which was something I'd never done before. It was embarrassing having such limited experience of everyday living like this, and was yet another legacy of my misspent youth.

◆ ◆ ◆

I've spoken to groups of prisoners about the issue of 'starting again,' on many occasions, and used the ancient story of The Prodigal Son to make my point. For those of you unfamiliar with it, let me briefly explain. A father had two sons, the younger of whom demanded his share of the inheritance. Upon receiving it he immediately left home and set about spending it on riotous living, (something most prisoners can relate to). Eventually he ran out of money and his friends deserted him, therefore he ended up feeding pigs in poverty and oftentimes wanted to eat the very husks he fed to the animals. Finally, coming to his senses, he made the brave and humble decision to return home to face his father and apologise. In a sense, that is exactly what I had to do with my own life: come back and start all over again. It was sometimes humiliating to stutter along in a learner car when younger men sped by, or to have never had a proper job, bank account, passport, or even paid a bill. I told the men that all their best thinking had landed them in the pig sty; they were covered in shit and needed to admit it. There was no way they could make it into the future unless they changed the thinking that put them in the shit in the first place.

"Instead of acting like a smart-arse, perhaps it's time you faced up to reality," I'd say, challenging them. "You're not clever and have acted stupidly. Maybe it's time to take the journey home, back to your beginnings and start again?"

During one such meeting at the Verne Prison in Portland, a black man from Brixton raised his hand, and politely asked, "Jimmy, if I do this, who will help me?"

I knew at once that he was convinced by what I'd said, and he looked ready to give up his futile pride and start again.

"That's a very good question," I admitted, nodding at him, "but I have no clear answer, except to say, if you were to make such a move, special people will come out of the woodwork to encourage and help. Life itself will assist you. This world has a way of knowing when a person humbles themselves; it carries an unmistakable 'feel' about it, and the world responds to it. After all, who can help a 'know all'?

"It can be as simple as this: perhaps you are standing at a bus stop on a rainy day, going to college. An old lady, a neighbour, may touch the back of your hand and say, 'Don't give up son.' Such moments are of great value and urge us forward. The next blessing is on its way, but we never know whether it consists of money, a bus pass, a weekend job, or that wonderful sense of being good and clean. We have to trust it, and trust life itself." Like many of the thousands I've spoken to, I sometimes wonder about that man from Brixton and what became of him.

The next big trip at work was a 127-mile canoe expedition along the Leeds to Liverpool canal, taking in 91 locks. Joanne Riley had kept in touch since the Scotland trip and soon volunteered to join in. When she accepted my invitation to come over a couple of days before the start in order to let me show her around Merseyside, I could hardly believe it.

I met her off the train at Liverpool's Lime Street Station and she looked great – and seemed as pleased to see me as I was her. After a quick bite to eat we set off for the movies and had a lot of fun watching Indiana Jones. It felt great having a good-looking female companion with whom I could share some meaningful conversation. During the show, I wanted to put my arm around her or give her a kiss but felt too afraid; my nerves were on edge. Later, while waiting at the bus stop, I somehow managed to pluck up enough courage to kiss her. Our embrace was mutual and we were glad to be together.

During the ride back, our conversation grew more intimate and I was able to share how I'd fallen for her in Scotland. She laughed in surprise. Having Joanne as a girlfriend sent me bursting with pride, I walked with a skip in my step and smiled from ear to ear. She told me how her circle of friends in Derbyshire, including her boyfriend, had grown stale and seemed to be heading nowhere. That's why she had joined 'The Wall' youth group in Chesterfield, to break free and reach higher goals. It took a lot of guts for her to join our Drake courses in a different county full of strangers, and I admired her for it.

On the canoe trip, it was hard to keep my distance from her; the Team Leader, Arthur was in his element, singing lullabies and making fun of us day and night. However, something I hadn't bargained for was the emergence of fiery underlying insecurities that bubbled up alongside the love I felt for Joanne. I liked to keep my emotions well under control but she, by her very presence, could drag them all up. It was tiresome battle having to wrestle with it all.

In the end, despite the heartache of putting her back on the train to Derbyshire, in some ways I was glad to see her go, because at least life would become a little less complicated! Upon returning home Joanne learnt that she'd been accepted at a college in Wrexham to study a degree in Youth and Community. It was great news, and brought her within visiting distance of me. We often met halfway in the beautiful city of Chester for a day out.

As the weather turned colder and the courses became more challenging, I had to focus harder on my job. The Team Leader needed me to remain strong and alert, therefore it stung me to be reprimanded by Dougie for coming in late a couple of times. Soon after, I was questioned about my attitude, which the team said had slipped. Their criticism hurt my feelings, making me defensive and angry, but I managed to accept their words, apologised and pledged to make a greater effort. The truth was, my mind had become so filled with Joanne that I wasn't paying attention to much else.

In many ways, the honeymoon period at work was over. I was having to handle challenging groups, run dangerous rock-climbing and abseiling sessions, organise kayaking trips, take people sailing, teach basic skiing and lead general mountaineering. The onset of winter meant I had to spend hundreds of pounds on new equipment, and Dougie also reminded me of the need to gain a driving licence. Almost two months' worth of my pay had already been spent on a series of driving lessons, in fact, for a few months, the job cost me more than I was being paid, but the expenditure was a worthwhile investment. Having no driving licence was yet another annoying legacy of my past; it seemed I was constantly rebuilding and catching up on things I'd neglected as a younger man.

Shortly after, I failed my first driving test by a whisker, but I didn't worry too much because I knew I'd pass sooner or later. However, Dougie saw things very differently and warned me that if I failed next time around, I'd be out of a job because driving mini-buses was an essential requirement of the job. I knew he was serious because he had sacked our store man, Rossi, for exactly the same thing. Suddenly the pressure was on.

During my walk to work in the mornings, an element introduced itself into my routine that always induced gratitude for the life I was living. Up ahead, through the maze of rush-hour traffic a coach would appear on the flyover and slowly snake its way toward me along Conway Street. Nobody took much notice of it on those cold mornings, but I knew that every man in the middle section was handcuffed together. It was the Risley bus! Prison officers were transporting them to court from that notorious Remand Centre where I'd suffered so much pain.

The men would be enjoying their anonymous trip through the streets, keeping an eye out for familiar faces or attractive women to admire, before being locked beneath the courts for the day. They would have been brought from their cells amidst banging doors and shouts early in the morning, to be herded into that ugly cage in the reception area. They'd get changed into their musty-smelling clothes and be given a bowl of watery porridge, which everybody tried to eat: there was a superstition among prisoners that said, 'If you don't eat your porridge on the last morning, you'd be back to eat it another day.' I knew the look in their eyes and the ache in their hearts as I stood in a shop doorway and watched as they passed me by. It was a good stick from which to measure how far I'd come since those mean old days.

◆ ◆ ◆

On Joanne's next visit we talked about getting married. I had a good job, we loved each other and certainly wanted to spend our lives together. Neither of us could see the point in having a long, drawn-out engagement and wanted to be married within about four months. In making our enquiries we discovered that the mission wasn't registered to perform weddings so we'd have to marry legally at the registry office, followed by the blessing of a church service separately. Finding a place to live would be the next thing to do; it made sense to buy a little house and my wages would cover the mortgage quite easily.

The numerous estate agents had plenty of properties to throw at us, but we soon became bored with the tiresome business of making appointments and viewing. We just wanted to have fun and therefore neglected viewings until after a while, neither of us were doing anything. Feeling guilty about my apathetic approach, I ventured out alone on my bike one afternoon for another look. Once again, I soon lost interest and found myself taking a shortcut back through the estate to the flat. However, on my way down Paterson Street a nice little end-terrace house caught my eye. It wasn't for sale but I rode in circles in a bit of a daydream looking at it and thinking, "That type of house would suit us fine." Once more, the feeling about the house was coming from deep down inside, just like the time I was told to 'Go to the office,' – a strange 'knowing'.

During Joanne's next visit we agreed to give the house-hunting another go. While walking through the town centre we called at the first estate agent's we came across, and as we closed the door behind us, the lady at the desk spoke up with enthusiasm. "Hello. I think I've got just the thing for a young couple like you."

It was one of those strange moments that I've grown accustomed to over the years, when time seems to stand still and you know exactly what's going to happen next. Before we had a chance to tell her our budget, or what we were looking for, she laid a folder upon the desk, and there before me was a picture of the little end-terrace house I'd been glued to the previous week.

"What do you think?" the lady asked.

It was far more than a coincidence to be offered it in this way.

"Is this house at the bottom end of Paterson Street?" I asked, just to make sure.

"Yes, it is," she answered. "It isn't quite finished yet – we're showing it privately and you'll be the first."

"What do you think Jimmy?" asked Joanne. "Worth a visit?"

"We don't need to visit it, I know it's the house for us."

"You can't just make an offer without even looking at it," said Joanne, staring at me as if I were crazy.

"Okay, we'll look, but I feel sure about this house."

Once outside, I was able to tell Joanne about the sequence of events that led to that particular house. With each step, I was becoming more convinced that 'life' itself was manoeuvring on our behalf in order to shape our immediate future. Back into my mind came the messages, 'within these streets', and the subsequent, 'go to the office', that led to the job. After taking a look at the house, we made an offer and began what seemed to us the complicated matter of getting a mortgage. The agency told us to expect the keys within a couple of months, maybe sooner.

It was pleasing to have that hurdle out of the way, but before we knew it, another obstacle presented itself: my driving test. The pressure on me was tremendous because everything suddenly hinged upon whether I passed or failed. No licence meant no job, which in turn meant no house or wedding. Everything could collapse!

On the eve of the test my nerves were a bit shot; I kept imagining making stupid mistakes and failing again. It was a nightmare. As I considered those destructive thoughts and where they were coming from, it occurred to me that it was my mind that was causing all the trouble, by constantly coming up with negative scenarios. I'd already completed all the driving manoeuvres perfectly well on numerous occasions and knew that I was fully capable of passing my test. I therefore rose up against those negative lies.

> ...i revisit this important episode in my new book, 'another kind of knowing'...in reality it was my ego that attacked the idea of me passing that driving test...

remember, the ego is the mind's idea
of who you are...it may surprise you
to know that your hidden ego might
have a very low opinion of you...

...in my case, taking a course of action
that would elevate my status in society,
above what my ego considered me
to be worth, caused it to attack...

Opposing all that internal negativism became an important key for future development in my life. The part of me that argued against the opposition was in fact my 'true inner self,' and the part that opposed me was my ego. To clarify, when I described the 'robot' I was imprisoned by in Grendon, the robot was in fact my ego. The ego is a framework of who our mind thinks we are and it fights to retain the false identity that it has created. The prospect of me passing my driving test would elevate me above what the ego thought I was worth, therefore it fought against the idea. However, as I felt the pain of internal opposition, my 'true inner self' stood back, observed what was going on, and spoke up in my defence.

It may alarm you to realise, that the greatest opponent to your progress in life is in fact your own mind. It would be difficult to explain in detail such an important human dynamic at this juncture of my story, but if you are interested in further reading, I address it more openly in my next book, *Another Kind of Knowing*. I also recommend *The Power of Now* by Eckhart Tolle, an excellent book.

Meanwhile, having put down the spiteful ego attack, the following morning I set off for my test with an air of positive expectation. Thankfully the examiner, unlike the previous one, seemed quite amiable and even managed a smile. I got off to a good start by running through the gears smoothly, operating the car with composure and kept my eye upon the dreaded rear-view mirror. When after five minutes I noticed him taking more notice of women walking down the street than my driving, I knew I was on to a winner. However, at the end, despite completing what I thought was a perfect test, it was impossible to tell by the examiner's demeanour whether I'd passed or failed.

After scribbling in his pad, he turned to me and said, "Mr. Rice, I'm pleased to say you've passed your test." I couldn't believe my ears! I could have kissed the man and ran a lap of honour around car! The relief was incredible and I could hardly wait to get back and tell Joanne. When I arrived, she was leaning over the balcony of the flats looking down onto the street, waiting. I tried to remain straight faced in order to keep her guessing, but as our eyes met, my joy broke out into a big smile and with clenched fists raised, I said, "I've done it!" I wasn't likely to forget the negative opposition that arose from within myself before that test, or the fact that I could stand up to it and win.

Meanwhile, there was no time to waste. I had to catch a train to South Wales in order to join up with the team who were working with a group in the Brecon Beacons. Before boarding, I phoned Dougie and thanked him for kicking my backside.

After a few trips to South Wales, I returned with a bout of genuine flu that put me in bed for almost two weeks. It was highly frustrating being laid up because nothing usually held me back; my middle name was energy! During endless days of shivering, sweating, drinking bottles of Lucozade and eating tubs of ice cream, I also grew impatient about our wedding arrangements. The keys to the house were due to be handed over within a couple of weeks, and I wanted to have the registry office side of things completed quickly so we could move in. I asked Joanne to go ahead and book the first available date.

My actions showed what little concept I had of family expectations, how much others would like to have been involved or how traditional they may have wished things to be. When I think back, there were faint voices, such as Peter and Sheila, trying to slow me down, but I had a strong personality and did things at my own pace. To me, the formalities were obstacles that needed to be overcome, nuisances blocking my path.

On Valentine's Day 1985, we entered the registry office with a small band of witnesses and quietly sealed our marriage, then two weeks later we visited the solicitor to collect the keys for our house. It was a real thrill for us to get them. I'd borrowed a van from work in order for us to move in straight away; our few possessions were able to fill the back of the small minibus quite easily. Besides our clothes, all we had was a bed, lamp, toaster, kettle, radio cassette, desk and some furniture. Despite being a small, two bedroomed terrace it still looked fairly empty after we moved in. We bought a table and some chairs, but still had to get toiletries, curtains, carpets and a cooker. We also had to have the gas switched on and a phone installed.

It was a nightmare of complications, the likes of which I'd never tackled before. I was useless at putting up curtain rails or repairing things, often dropping tools and clasping my head in exasperation. As well as this, money had to be put aside for incoming bills, leaving us with less spare cash than ever. My habit of carrying a pocket full of notes soon had to stop as money just seemed to slip through my fingers at that time.

At work, I was having to learn, at home I was having to learn and in life I was having to learn, and sometimes the whole thing clashed with my pride. I longed for the day when my abilities in all departments of life became more fully developed, but it was a long way off.

Our marriage service soon came around, during which we had our union blessed by the pastor and made our vows publicly before God. It was a superb day. A great collection of friends and family joined together in wishing us well and every chair was filled. We were presented with all sorts of beautiful gifts and cards. Two special guests were Gerry and Annette, who'd travelled all the way up from Grendon. Afterwards, a whole crowd of folk came back for a look at the house, filling it to the rafters. Their bustling presence sealed a beginning for us in that place; our married life had really begun.

The wedding was arranged to coincide with our Easter break, which enabled us to spend two weeks travelling around having fun together as our honeymoon. After that, I returned to work and Joanne to college, where she stayed for two nights each week. I missed her on those occasions but it was important for her to finish her studies.

CHAPTER 9

Rollercoaster Living

With me working away so much, Joanne often came home to an empty house. On one occasion, she found the place had been burgled. Fear and insecurity immediately gripped her; she was alone in a relatively strange, crime-ridden area. Her instinctive reaction was to contact me through Dougie at the office, but being a former Marine with a wife who'd been through plenty of similar experiences, Dougie set about calming her down. One of the girls from the office stayed with Joanne overnight, while everybody else kept in close contact during the few days before my return. Fortunately, the burglar didn't cause any damage. It had been a quick job, with just two pieces of electrical equipment taken, probably the work of a junkie looking for easy money.

It was the first time I'd fully considered Joanne's position of being a long way from home in a town full of strangers. Even worse, I was due to be home for only two nights as it was one of those rare occasions when we did back-to-back courses completely away from our area. Jo and I stayed close together during that short period and on the day of my departure I could find no words to comfort her. What could I say? We bought two sets of stationary with stamps and promised to write to one-another every day.

With a full rucksack on my back, I turned to her on the doorstep and said, "I'm sorry, Jo. You know I have to go." At that, I crossed the street, disappeared through the alley-way opposite and submerged into the housing estate. It was a fairly unhappy Jimmy Rice who travelled up to Scotland that day with a particularly rowdy group, all set to build another bridge. I sent Jo a card from a motorway service station in order for her to receive something quickly. The real letter writing began late that night while I sat up in my sleeping bag leaning against the wall of the large equipment store in the Highlands.

Trying to occupy a dozen street-wise young men that week was difficult enough without the terrible weather conditions that descended upon us. We had to abandon the bridge project after three futile days of having it washed away, and concentrate on other tasks. Some of the group went out culling deer with the ranger while the others planted trees, laid paths and undertook a variety of jobs. It was a little unsatisfying because, unlike building a bridge, there was little to show for our efforts.

An important element on the courses was the inclusion of young women. Their presence brought a much better balance to the group dynamic and prevented male rowdiness from getting out of hand. Unfortunately, on that occasion we were unable to recruit any females, so the jokes grew dirtier, interaction more aggressive and attitudes bullish. Included on that particular course was a young man from somewhere on the European mainland, accompanied by an instructor from London who was there to look after him. The European was highly educated, apparently the illegitimate son of a foreign King, and related to the family of a world-famous painter. Unfortunately, like many of our volunteers, he'd taken to drugs and made something of a mess of his privileged upbringing. My boss called me from London to explain why he was there and asked that I take special care of him: "We're doing a favour for some very important people, Jim," he told me. However, when the course began, I'm sure the young fellow must have wondered what had hit him.

I had lots of crazy team games lined up that we played in order for everybody to get to know each other quickly, but he found it difficult to 'lower' himself and join in properly. As soon as the other lads heard his posh accent, noticed he had a minder and sensed his superior attitude, he became the butt of every joke – I'll leave it to your imagination regarding the sort of things they called him!

After complaining to me I said, "Sink or swim sunshine. If you watch them closely, they're as rough with each other as they are with you. It's just the way they are."

Thankfully, he slowly turned out to be a good sport and did all he could to give as good as he was getting, triumphantly referring to us as, 'a bunch of Philistines'. The lads winked at each other and pretended they didn't know what a Philistine was. While driving through the Scottish Highlands, during a tea-break, one of the lads pushed him into a nearby river. His minder ran across to see what was happening and only narrowly escaped being thrown straight in behind him. As we fished him out, I had a funny mental picture of my boss reassuring the lad's parents that, "Jimmy Rice is a good man and will take good care of your son," yet unbeknown to them he was being dragged sopping wet out of a freezing cold river. Luckily, we dried him up quickly, gave him a change of clothes and he didn't take it too badly.

As the days rolled by, he pulled his sleeves up and got on with things despite the rough conditions and we all started to like him quite a lot. It was almost sad to see how fond he grew of our rough and tumble guys; all of whose lives were very poor compared to his. One of the funniest moments came on the morning before going out hunting with the local ranger, when the group gave him a very special present. As we climbed out of the mini-bus they handed it to him and I don't think I'll ever forget his uncontrollable laughter. He laughed so hard we all ended up in hysterics with him. Attached to a helmet for him to wear during the hunt (in which gunmen roamed all around), were two very prominent antlers. He was intelligent enough to realise that the guys had really taken to him, despite the barbed humour of making him a target for every rifle in the area. I still have a photograph of him wearing it.

Quite by accident, a situation arose one evening that knocked the frustration out of our working conditions. One of the instructors had a friendly wrestling match on the straw-covered concrete floor with one of the volunteers. Under the care-free eye of a 'referee' perched high upon a stack of crates under the dim lights, they crashed around until utterly exhausted. Next, another instructor grappled with a different scallywag, crashing through fence-posts, and gasping for breath until once again, they both lay on the ground panting for breath. In the midst of the groaning, shouting, sweat and dust, we found ourselves naturally split into two groups, instructors at one end of the big hut and volunteers at the other. Each group took turns in allowing one of their group to select an opponent from the other. The level of noise was fantastic as each team shouted their man on, and of course, the greatest roar of all came when our European friend chose to fight with his minder. I'm sure he'd never had so much fun in his whole life.

It was hilarious how we all adopted the exaggerated behaviour of TV wrestlers, threatening the opposing team with shouts and exaggerated gestures while the fighters, stripped down to their jeans, rolled and scraped their way around the floor into hay bales and boxes while trying to get the better of each other.

I had four contests, two of which against a big fellow from Derbyshire called Dave, who looked like a Red Indian and was as strong as an ox. It took a submission or shoulders pin-down to win, but neither of us could quite get the better of the other. All our fights ended in total exhaustion, with both of us having to crawl from the ring. After what seemed like hours, everybody drifted away to flop onto their sleeping bags, thirsty, covered with dust, scrapes, bruises and ripped clothing. It turned out to be the salvation of that particular course, and made the final few days a lot of fun.

A steady flow of letters arrived from Joanne while I was there, each filled with the news of how her faith increased in strength each day. Perhaps the burglary was a blessing in disguise? She quoted sections of the Bible that had almost jumped off the page as she read them, each containing promises of care and protection. In her hours of need she was making the fantastic discovery of her own spirituality, and finding it could be relied upon.

The obstacle of time that separated me from going home held similar frustrations to those I'd experienced in prison. I wanted to run back to Joanne's rescue and deliver her from all anxiety, but through her letters I became aware of heaven's hand wanting to do the job itself. The Joanne I returned to was one who'd taken her first steps into a personal faith, away from being tossed around by the fears of the mind in meaningless directions. A part of her that had previously relied on me now had its trust in the heavens.

As we drifted into another summer, Joanne and I became increasingly involved in the Sunday School run by the old ladies at the mission. Despite their genuine love for the kids, the ladies' strength and health had seen better years, and the load had become too much of a strain. We bounced onto the scene bringing youthful enthusiasm, and utilised a few helpers we recruited. After a few months, the ladies dropped out completely, leaving us to it.

Many of the kids came from homes in which they were exposed to high levels of crime and violence, along with alcohol and drug misuse. Most were from unemployed one-parent families who walked a thin line between destitution and manageable debt; the bread line in every sense of the word. As the children arrived at the mission each Sunday, a gang of compatriots often arrived to threaten them with violence, pulling some away at the doors and spitting on others as they entered. Older ones clambered all over the roof, hanging down to gesticulate through the windows while others sneaked in to try to cause damage. People living nearby saw what was happening, but fear of retribution forced them into silence – nobody reported anything. Eventually they completely ruined things and for the safety of the poor children who attended, we had to shut it down. Curiously, a few years after writing the first edition of this book, I was conducting a talk in a prison when a hard-bitten young man asked to speak to me.

"I was one of the people in your book who ruined the Sunday School," he said, looking very embarrassed, "and I just want to say sorry."

I felt sad for him because his life had taken such a predictable path of failure.

"No problem mate," I answered. "It's all in the past now."

He told me he'd listened avidly to my talk and had obviously read my book, and like so many I've known, I wonder what became of him?

At work, I was thrilled when Joanne was given permission to join me on an expedition to the French Pyrenees, as wives were not usually allowed. We'd often talked about visiting the Alps or other big mountain ranges, therefore the Pyrenees with its peaks doubling the size of anything in Britain was a wish come true. As the trip coincided with Joanne's birthday we agreed it would be her present (but secretly I had bought her a gold chain and kept it hidden in my rucksack.)

Several weeks before departure our team leader resigned, which left Kenny and I to organise everything until a suitable replacement could be found. Having to take full responsibility brought us to a whole new level of awareness.

The Pyrenees group we selected for the trip were great fun, and it was a fitting reward for the huge strides they'd taken in life. Their songs and laughter made the long drive through England and France seem short. We rested at a camp on the edge of Limoges on the way south, before hitting the heart of the Pyrenees the following day.

Our camp was situated in the Ossau Valley beneath the towering peak of Pic du Midi d'Ossau, 2,884 metres (9,461 feet). Along the other side ran a deep gorge where we had great fun jumping into deep pools and swimming around. A game we played was to follow an instructor as he climbed across the walls above the pools, the penalty for falling being a big cold splash.

My group decided to take a day off sunbathing before embarking upon our main objective – a six-day circular expedition across the mountains into Spain and back. The first day of trekking awakened everybody to the reality of walking in big country. Through blistering heat, we trudged uphill for five hours before crossing a saddle, (a path between two peaks), then settling down for lunch. Nobody walked far that day without drinking heavily from their water bottles and draping soaking wet tee-shirts over their heads. Joanne found the challenge quite difficult and soon began to struggle badly, but fortunately, I was strong enough to carry a lot of her equipment. Usually, people found their legs after a couple of days, but poor Jo never really got into her stride. Each evening when people swam in the mountain lakes or chatted over cooking stoves, Joanne lay exhausted inside her tent. It was unusual for her; she kept herself fit and was quite a gritty character, however after a few bouts of morning sickness, we later discover why it had been so hard!

The expedition itself had many wonderful moments that stayed in my mind for a long time after. There were the breathtaking views, amazing wildlife, huge eagles and incredible sunsets. The sense of peace and wellbeing that enveloped the group defied description – everybody was very chilled.

Day five saw three of us split off from the group to see what we could find at a mountain chalet we'd spotted on the map; beside that, the whole area was deserted. Mercifully, after a long walk, we found it and entered like starving cowboys having crossed a desert. The little Brazilian lady who ran the place fetched us bowls of ice cream and plenty of cold drinks, followed by the delights of French fries, omelets and hot coffee. Such luxury made it incredibly hard to get up and resume the rigours of the course. We bought two big crates of beer and a few bottles of wine for the group, then set about carting it down the valley for the others. The Brazilian lady was horrified that we should attempt carrying such a heavy weight and offered to give us a ride in her car along a narrow track to the end of the valley. It was a massive relief to climb into her tiny car and set off along the twisting path. I noticed her legs were so short that wooden blocks had been attached to the pedals.

"Belle vallée," I commented, making small talk about the beautiful valley as she drove along. However, as she looked at me to answer, the car drifted dangerously towards an enormous drop, before she managed to snatch it back under control. We were all gripping our seats in fear, but the lady drove on as if nothing had happened. A few minutes later I made the mistake of instinctively speaking to her again, and

134

regretted it as soon as the words crossed my lips. Once more she looked across to answer while the car skimmed the edge of the road.

"Jimmy!" hissed the lads in the back seat, their eyes boring a hole in the back of my head.

The lady continued driving along, smiling, oblivious to the near heart seizures taking place all around, until we reached the end of the valley. The lads scrambled out quickly to unpack the goods while I stayed and chatted to the lady for a few moments. Remembering it was Joanne's birthday in a couple of days, I arranged with her to supply a cake with candles and we'd return to her chalet after the expedition for a surprise party.

Meanwhile, the group was in a victorious mood after almost completing the expedition. We lit a big fire and sat around drinking, eating, singing, dancing and generally having a good time until the early hours. Then, one by one, everybody drifted off to sleep soundly in their sleeping bags. In the morning, as the sun rose above the surrounding crags, I awoke to the comical picture of empty bottles stuffed into crates, a fire smoldering lightly and everybody scattered around in the open air fast asleep.

It was with relative ease that we completed the final day and slumped triumphantly into our tents at base camp. That evening, after a good wash and change of clothes, we set off in the mini-bus for the chalet. It was lovely to be dressed in comfortable clothing without the dreaded rucksack for company. We looked a very healthy bunch, our bronzed skin glowing against the bright colors of our cotton shirts. At the chalet, we feasted to our hearts' content around a big table, each toasting the others' success in completing the expedition. A number of French people arrived to fill the remaining seats and we all shared plenty of laughter. The Brazilian lady dug out some old Beatles music for everybody to sing to, and it turned into the rowdiest night the place had ever seen.

Halfway through proceedings, I sneaked into the kitchen to light the candles on the cake, then the Brazilian lady dimmed the lights and bought it in ablaze. Joanne cheered with everybody else, wondering whose birthday it was, until the cake came her way and everybody turned to cheer her. The surprise brought tears to her eyes as we roared out a chorus of Happy Birthday. Joanne's bewilderment was further increased when I produced a gold chain and fastened it around her neck. Everybody insisted we dance together and cheered as we moved slowly across the floor. We began to kiss but broke off, laughing, as wolf whistles filled the air. It was a great night that neither of us will ever forget.

The following morning, a small group of us took the opportunity to set off early and climb the nearby Pic di Midi d'Ossau, while the others slept soundly. It was the highest peak I'd ever climbed and my first experience of the effects of altitude. After scrambling the final few hundred yards to the top I was out of breath, but instead of regaining it fairly quickly like usual, I continued breathing heavily for the whole time we were up there.

Sitting on top of that mountain with such breathtaking views all around, I was filled with gratitude for the way in which my life had turned around – it seemed almost impossible. However, along with such unspeakable joy, I couldn't help but feel sad for the fate of the many others I'd known, who were trapped in a spiral of destruction and failure. "Why me?" I wondered. "How did I overcome so very much?"

We sat there for quite a long time until a sudden chill in the air warned me of a possible change in the weather. Out of nowhere, small clouds gathered against the far horizon, therefore we wasted no time in descending. At one point, I appreciated all of my training when encountering a steep drop onto a path that differed from the one on which we had climbed. Using all the right knots and techniques, I found a good anchor point and lowered the other members to safer ground before abseiling down to join them. No sooner had I coiled the rope than the heavens opened and poured with rain. I was so glad to have chosen the right moment to descend, otherwise the high rocks would have been treacherous.

Once back at camp we all ate together and decided to set off very early the next morning in order to spend a day in Paris on the way back. It was another long drive, during which Joanne's health started to play up again, and she felt sick for most of the journey. After camping at a seedy site on the edge of the city, we took to the streets for a long walk through the major sights. The wide, pedestrianised avenues were filled with tourists from all over the world, beating paths through mile after mile of traders and pavement artists, all vying for cash.

My mind was cast back almost two years to my experiences on those familiar Parisian streets. Genevieve's parting words, "Go back to your God," rang afresh in my ears. There was Denny, too, with that crooked, scornful smile breaking out across a cheeky face that masked a struggle between madness and sadness. We'd virtually lost touch, but I still wanted to see him again.

During the afternoon, Joanne and I set off to look around his old haunts in an effort to find him, but in a city so big, busy, frantic and ever- changing, our effort was like a drop in the ocean. After an hour we gave up, rejoined the group on the tourist trail and before too long, headed back to the minibus in the evening.

The journey home was long and hard, Kenny alternating the driving with me in a non-stop shuttle while everybody slouched uncomfortably against one another trying to sleep. Coming home was always difficult; throughout the years I spent working on Drake courses it never got any easier. Spending time in beautiful areas like the Pyrenees, Scotland,

North Wales, the Lake District or the Yorkshire Dales made city life seem uglier than ever.

Within a week of arriving home, it was indeed confirmed that Joanne was pregnant, which of course explained why she'd found the Pyrenees trip so difficult. We were very excited by the news and immediately began buying baby clothes and reading material about what to expect. Joanne continued at college for as long as she could, but after seven months of pregnancy she had to stop. It signaled the end of her degree, which was an indication of our immaturity in terms of planning for the future.

◆ ◆ ◆

It was around this period when I started to realise that a curious power emanated from me when I shared my story with people. A young fellow from work came to visit our house one day and sat looking uncomfortable. I didn't know what he wanted but after describing how his life had become a mess, I heard myself ask, "What are you looking for, Phil?"

"I don't know."

"Do you want your life to be rescued like mine?" I asked.

"Yeah, I do," he answered, looking me squarely in the eye.

I had no idea what to do, but laid my hand upon his shoulder and asked that he may experience the same life-changing force that I had. Suddenly, he was in floods of tears, weeping uncontrollably and crying out for heaven's help. It was incredible to watch him go through that experience. He had all sorts of visions springing up in his mind.

He then sat in a big armchair clutching a Bible for two days saying, "God's in this house. I'm staying." We lived around him until he felt able to leave, but not until we'd convinced him that eternal 'life' would be with him no matter where he went. He seemed to think God was actually present in our house.

138

The day after Phil left, a young married mother from our street called around and seemed very much on edge as we chatted. Then, with the same feeling I'd had about Phil, I said, "Julie, do you want to be transformed right now?"

"Oh, yes, I do!" she blurted out. Then with her head in her hands, she wept great sobs while crying out to heaven. Like Phil, she passed through an amazing experience into a new life, but I wasn't exactly sure how it had happened.

Joanne and I wondered what might happen next as these incidents had caught us completely by surprise. Two days later, we got a visit from Michael, a strange young man who attended the church from time to time and spent his days walking the streets. All previous conversations I'd tried to spark up with him had been like flogging a dead horse; he was deep and very unhappy. That night though, he seemed a little more talkative and before long, the same urge arose within me to ask him the same question I'd ask the others: "Michael, do you want your life to be transformed tonight?"

"Yes," he answered, quite definitely. He wanted to pray but as hard as he tried, something inside kept making him angry. In an effort to help, I prayed for him and as I did, something invisible seemed to lift off his back and pass across mine. It was horrible. Although I'd heard about spiritual darkness, I'd never come across anything overtly evil, at least not until then. Michael left the house feeling as pent-up in the prison of his own mind as when he'd arrived. It had been an interesting week, with two people unexpectedly coming into the light and another seemingly unable to break out of his spiritual entanglements.

Once in a while I was asked to share my story at small gatherings, and judging by the reaction, I began to realise that my experiences were quite unusual. Occasionally whilst walking with individuals through beautiful countryside in my job, I'd be asked about my life; most people assumed I was university educated and had a good background. I never told anybody my story unless pressed for it, and even then, I was reluctant. However, whenever I spoke of it, they invariably refused to believe me and thought I was having a joke. When finally accepting that I was telling the truth, they found it very difficult to grasp because I'd changed so much from the younger man I described to them. When I overcame the ego that so dominated my life while in Grendon Prison, up from my midst sprang a whole new life that had been waiting to get out. That new life had a glow about it that has affected people around me ever since my transformation.

During public talks, I'd sometimes ask whether anybody would like to come forward at the end of a meeting, and as I reached out to take hold of their outstretched hand, some would collapse unconscious on the floor or others would burst into uncontrollable tears, as if their whole body of pain were pouring out all over the floor in front of everybody. Things like that have happened more times than I could ever count, and it's always been a struggle to explain why they happened.

Like most people who adopt a faith, be it Christian, Muslim, Hindu or Judaism, I tried to cram my experiences into the one I had adhered to, but I found the vastness of the heavens and all its variations impossible to be contained within a single creed. Consider this: the very 'mind' we use to understand eternal 'life' is incapable of doing so. In fact, it is only by dropping the mind that the heavens can be experienced at all. I will try to explain what I mean by a simple story involving Jesus.

One day a rich young ruler tracked Jesus down and asked, "How may I inherit eternal life?" The young fellow hungered for the beautiful freedom that Jesus exuded, and heard that others were experiencing it too. The only thing obstructing anybody from experiencing that special 'life' is their egoic mind. As with all enlightened people, Jesus could not make the heavens known by explaining them, but did the next best thing and pointed to that which was blocking it. "Go, sell everything you have, give it to the poor and follow me," he said. At that, the young man walked away grieving, because he was wealthy. He was completely identified with his possessions and was too afraid to break with them. In effect, Jesus' message was simply, 'Break with your egoic identity (in the young man's case, being a rich property owner) and the newness of life will arise uninterrupted from within you.'

The mind cannot conceive of anything beyond the bounds of its own comprehension. In effect it says, "I can't see it, I don't understand it, therefore, it cannot exist." The human mind is utterly blind to the spirit or consciousness realm and therefore considers it foolishness. It's impossible to be governed by two differing principles at the same time, therefore, if the individual is identified with their egoic occupation, class status, nationality, background – or just about anything in the natural world – it will keep them from being identified with the light of 'life.' The mystics describe such a state as, being 'asleep'.

In my case, it was the reservoir of eternal 'life' within me that was having an effect on people's lives. The reservoir of 'life' within them responded to mine. Many were also moved by the first edition of this book, but I don't know how, except to say that if a person seeks, they will surely find. I received countless letters from all over the world, written by prisoners on scraps of paper in the middle of dark nights. They spoke of 'seeing the light,' and 'coming to their senses,' of 'finding new hope,' and 'finally laying hold of what they had always been looking for'. I loved receiving those letters, so filled with honest emotion, amazing stories and fresh hope.

◆ ◆ ◆

Meanwhile, back at work our new team leader had arrived, Nick Gannicliffe, a man under whom I would grow considerably over the following 18 months. Unlike so many insecure leaders who hogged their position, Nick allowed me into the decision-making process at every opportunity. This drew out my strengths as a leader and also highlighted weaknesses where training was required. It was a refreshing partnership that helped me approach the job in a far more professional light. In addition, Fairbridge Drake, as it became known, was a national charity with teams in many big cities and was becoming increasingly thorough in its safety procedures as each year passed, so if I was to gain future promotion I'd have to remain proficient in the full range of outdoor pursuits.

Arriving home from work one evening, Joanne told me she'd been having regular contractions all afternoon. Although she had been pregnant for nine months, it suddenly dawned on me that I was about to become a father! We settled down for the evening, keeping track of the intervals between contractions until eventually deciding to go to the hospital. We were very excited. It was a long night, watching the monitor, helping Joanne breathe easily and comforting her as much as I was able. The process went on and on into the early hours until eventually, the doctor came in to deliver our lovely little daughter, Sarah Jane, weighing in at 8lb 9oz and in perfect health.

Joanne's mother, who'd driven over from Nottingham, waited anxiously in the corridor for news and when I eventually stepped outside to tell her, I burst into tears on her shoulder. It had all been too much. Joanne needed a week in hospital before being allowed home and when she was released, I took two weeks off work to look after them both.

It was incredible how this tiny person came along and completely took over our lives. We listened out for her every noise, provided every possible comfort and cared until it ached.

The presents, cards, visits, phone calls and well wishes from work, church, family and friends came like a flood. We didn't realise how many people we knew. However, just a few days before my return to work, Joanne began haemorrhaging badly and an ambulance was called to rush her back into hospital. My poor wife had already been through so much, and now this. I was left holding little Sarah in a hospital room while they wheeled Joanne away for an emergency operation. In the confusion, I didn't know whether she'd live or die. The stress of the previous weeks had been hard enough to bear, but waiting in that half-lit room as the clock ticked by only made it worse.

After what seemed an age, a nurse appeared wearing a big smile; the operation had been a success and Joanne was fine. Having a baby enter our lives was a massive learning curve in and of itself, but with those added complications to contend with, our initial experience of childbirth wasn't entirely positive. While it took Joanne some time to regain her strength, little Sarah was bursting with the newness of life and she brought us so much joy. Owing to Joanne's delicate condition, my protective instincts for both her and the baby convinced me that we needed to change churches. There was another one nearby called Emmanuel that had several young families like ourselves. We knew a number of people there and I was already acquainted with the pastor, Roger.

Leaving the mission was an emotional pull, but it had to be done; it had been my first church and I'd begun to grow under their loving care. However, prior to our departure, an incident happened in our street that sent shockwaves right through my system. While sitting in our living room talking to Joanne with the baby resting on my knee, a thunderous crash nearly caved-in our front door. As I calmly passed the baby to Joanne, another crash hit it and my blood ran cold as I walked angrily down the hall. All I could think about was my tiny child, and Joanne still vulnerable from her operation.

I opened the door to see Michael leap forward, screaming at me. Instinctively, my fist hit him square in the face, knocking him backwards. After quickly throwing him to the ground and grabbing him tightly around the throat, I ordered him out onto the street. Then, before the neighbours had a chance to pull back their net curtains for a good look, I was up and walking back to our door, where Joanne now stood watching in shock. Suddenly, she screamed, "Jimmy, watch out!"

I turned to see Michael flying at me again, and this time thinking he had a knife, I knocked him semi-conscious with a volley of punches. The neighbours were at their windows as I dragged him back to his feet and sent him staggering down the street. They must have been wondering what kind of Christianity I was into, perhaps the John Wayne variety!

I walked back into the house feeling the sickness of adrenaline; it was hard to believe what has just happened. Not only was I supposed to avoid violence, I naively believed that by dint of my religious faith, nothing like this could ever happen. For two years I'd tried to help Michael, only for it to end with me flattening him. As a precaution, I called the police and explained my actions, but they assured me that everything was fine; they were getting reports of crack-pots kicking doors all the time.

...in general, life was moving along
very nicely...however, when it came to
my faith, i was having problems...

...what began as a beautiful
awakening came under attack...

...something extraordinary had
happened to me and i loved it...however,
the ego that i unseated in grendon fought
hard to regain its authority over me...

...this time it came in the guise of
religious knowledge and was hard to
identify, but i got there in the end...

CHAPTER 10

Growing Pains

An important lesson I had to learn from my encounter with Michael concerned time-wasters. Having helped many people over the years, I've often had to show a measure of tough honesty in equal measure to compassion. For example, while camped in the Yorkshire Dales with a group, I decided to walk up a long hill in the evening to watch the sun go down. A guy with a troubled background asked whether he could join me, so we walked together.

During our stroll, he asked a number of questions that led me to reveal that I was once a violent criminal. Such was his surprise that he pressed me further to find out what had changed me.

"My life had been in danger for quite some time," I said, "and after a year of intensive therapy, something in me broke. I cried out to God for help and things have never been the same since."

After walking quietly along for a while, he suddenly fell to his knees in the dust and began crying out to God to rescue his life too. As usual, the whole thing caught me by surprise; his tears were certainly genuine and he seemed to go through a very powerful spiritual experience.

Back in Birkenhead after the course was complete we unpacked the kit, issued certificates, then allowed everybody to go home. Later in the afternoon while I trying to finish my work the same guy returned, carrying all his belongings and told me his girlfriend had kicked him out. This immediately put me under pressure; I was tired after the course and wanted to get home to my wife. After giving him a cup of tea, I rang a friend, who said he might be able to find him a place in the hostel where he worked.

"What am I going to do?" The young man kept asking me, meaning: "What are you going to do?"

When we arrived at the hostel, it wasn't initially clear whether he'd be given a room or not. Then while we waited in the foyer, he said to me, "Why can't I come and stay at your house?"

Once again, I felt the twist of religious guilt regarding the poor and homeless, but after a pause I pulled him to one side and said, "Listen, Buster. I'm helping you as much as I can, but I know what you're trying to do. You want to push me so hard that I'll let you down, then you'll blame me and feel sorry for yourself. Well, don't go laying things on me, because it won't work. I'll help you stand on your own two feet if that's what you really want. So, what's it to be?"

He looked at me in wide-eyed amazement, then coyly admitted that he'd been trying it on. After that bit of straight talking, he perked up again. My friend and I secured him a room in the hostel and from there we began helping him get his life back together. I had to be tough with him in order to wake him up.

◆ ◆ ◆

18 months after Nick's arrival as Team Leader at work, he decided to resign and further his career with another

organisation in the Lake District. It was a sad loss because I'd flourished well under his leadership, becoming proficient in all aspects of the work. His departure would signal the arrival of a replacement. I had most of the qualities needed to do the job myself and considered applying for the position, but my formal qualifications were slightly incomplete.

I watched with interest the kind of people who began applying for the job and noticed that none of them were any more capable than myself. Therefore, in fear of coming under the leadership of somebody less skilled than myself, I decided to apply for the job. Joanne and I grew quite excited about the prospect of my promotion, as it would mean more money and add substance to my employment credentials.

The two major questions on the application form asked what personal qualities I'd bring to the position, along with what plans I had for the further development of our work with young people. At first glance they seemed like tricky questions, but when I thought about them, my mind suddenly burst with ideas just waiting to get out. Added to this was my genuine concern for the young people we worked with. I wanted to help them as much as I'd been helped myself. After pouring my ideas onto paper, I mailed the application to the Directors in London and hoped for the best.

When I received a letter inviting me to attend, I suddenly realised I'd never had a proper interview in my life. On the train journey to London I felt nervous, imagining the many questions they might ask. At our central office the two Directors, whom I knew quite well, welcomed me and got proceedings off to a quick start. Amazingly, they both thought my rehabilitation from crime was the sole result of taking part in a couple of Drake courses. In seeking to put them in the picture we spent almost two hours talking about spiritual matters!

To my surprise, the interview was very enjoyable and helped us get to know each other much better. Eventually, they asked me to wait outside their office for a while until they'd come to a decision. Sitting there alone waiting for an answer was uncomfortable to say the least and I couldn't bear the thought of them refusing me. However, the waiting didn't last for long; I think they'd already made up their minds. Soon they called me back inside, shook my hand and congratulated me on gaining the position.

I was absolutely thrilled, but immediately had the same feeling I'd experienced when originally given the instructor's job: the desperate need to get outside and breathe some fresh air. As soon as the pleasantries were over, I excused myself from the office and set off walking briskly around London's West End. What a relief to get the job! This was a big step forward in my march away from the past. I'd been out of prison for four years and things were going really well. Joanne was excited when I rang to pass on the good news – it was just the kind of encouragement we needed.

Before heading to Euston Station for the journey home, I called into a burger bar on Oxford Street for a bite to eat. Sitting there eating brought back memories of old. On many occasions, I'd walked along that street without money, feeling lonely and hungry. I'd envied those who had enough money to buy any food they wanted and sit eating with friends. As I looked out at the passers-by on that grey day I wondered whether somebody may be looking at me with the same sense of painful envy?

After boarding my train to Liverpool that evening, I fell into a very interesting conversation with a woman who sat opposite.

"You must be a Child Psychologist," I said to her, taking my seat without ever having met her in my life.

She was taken aback. "Sorry, do I know you?" she asked.

"No," I replied, without knowing how to explain. "I just know things and thought it would be interesting to chat. Fancy a drink? I'm going to the buffet bar."

After returning with food and drinks we spent the next two hours talking endlessly about all sorts of things, but she seemed to be far more interested in my journey through life than anything to do with her psychology. She was particularly interested in why I did my job, how my life had changed and why I helped so many people.

"Well it's not me, is it? It's God really," I said. "I think that's how it all works."

"Well, I understand that," she said, "but you did all the work. It was you who caused everything to happen. Surely you can see that?"

It was true that I'd wrung myself inside out in Grendon searching for answers, and faced up to many painful real-ities about myself. Also, when on my knees, having been challenged to crawl across the floor during the Psychodrama session, it was my own courage that made it happen. The destruction of my egoic identity, (or robot, as I called it at the time) was the most significant event of my entire life. Immediately upon toppling its power, eternal 'life' welled-up from within and I was never the same again. I was so grateful for this lady's clarity because I'd become increasingly con-fused about God and Christianity.

My primary concern was that believers attributed all the power, righteousness, glory, spirit and wonder to God alone. The problem with doing that was that it left the believer in a kind of useless vacuum, like a pawn in a heavenly game. Every time I told people at the church about somebody's life that had been dramatically changed following a conversation, or a public talk, they inferred that it had almost nothing to do with me.

"The goodness doesn't come from us," was the implica-tion, "but from God alone," which suggested there was no goodness in man worth giving. I was way too young in the faith to argue with anybody, certainly not God himself, but I hungered for more satisfactory answers.

CHAPTER 11

Fighting For Life

In the same way that I needed to gain a driving licence to fulfill my obligations as an instructor, I was now required to gain a Mountain Leadership Certificate to meet the requirements of a Team Leader. It was a difficult qualification to gain, beginning with at least two solid years of leadership experience documented in a log book, then five days' intensive training at an authorised centre, covering all aspects of the craft. Following the training a minimum period of a year had to elapse before embarking on the assessment, which included six full days of being tested in the mountains.

With over three years of continuous experience in leading groups and having completed my training, I was all set for the assessment and felt confident of passing. In order to be fully prepared, I arranged to visit North Wales and teach a friend all about night navigation for a couple of days before tackling the rigorous test. Teaching the subject was an ideal way of sharpening the skill. However, the day before we were due to depart, I felt some kind of bug that set my shoulders tingling and head aching. We postponed the trip for a day so I could get some antibiotics from the doctor. Illness never usually held me back, so I just ignored it and carried on.

The doctor couldn't find anything wrong and told me to take some mild painkillers and let him know how things progressed over the next 24 hours. That night I was kept wide awake by a throbbing headache mixed with severe feelings of flu. The doctor visited me the following day but still couldn't find exactly what was wrong. Therefore, he told me to continue with the painkillers and keep him informed.

On that second night, beside my throbbing head, I began vomiting violently. Two nights without sleep had left me feeling a wreck, but when the doctor heard that I'd been sick and unable to sleep a wink he rang for an ambulance to take me to hospital immediately. Despite feeling pretty rotten, I couldn't understand what all the fuss was about. Why the ambulance? When it arrived, two men brought a special chair to my bedroom, ready to carry me down the stairs.

"What's all this about?" I thought, putting on a brave face and getting ready to walk out by myself, but to my surprise, I couldn't stand, let alone walk. During the ride to the hospital and subsequent transfer to an isolation ward I grew worse. The nurses had to keep the room darkened because the light sent terrible pain through my head. Doctors arrived to carry out various tests in an effort to find out what my problem was, but nobody could figure it out.

That night I was filled with excruciating pain, rolling around the bed having delirious nightmares. One minute I was shaking uncontrollably with cold, the next almost suffocating with heat. My family visited, but I had no idea what they were talking about or what was going on. Meanwhile the doctors struggled to find out the cause of my illness and gave me a spinal tap, thinking I might have meningitis. I vomited everything that passed my lips, had needles poked into my veins day and night, couldn't urinate and was becoming thinner by the hour. Something terrible was eating away at me.

The main clue to the problem came after a few days when my calf muscles seized up, causing further agonising pain. Fortunately, the Tropical School of Medicine in Liverpool recognised the calf seizures as a key symptom associated with a disease called leptospirosis, or Weil's disease. Just five days after arriving in hospital my kidneys were failing, and the walls of my stomach began to collapse, causing me to vomit blood all over the bed. Clearly dying, I was moved into intensive care where all kinds of tubes were attached to various parts of my body. With my skin completely yellow, bones protruding because of my dramatic weight loss, I looked almost dead. Joanne, my family, my pastor and all those who knew me were in complete shock, because after just one week in hospital I was facing death.

My boss Dougie took it particularly badly after being told it was leptospirosis, and in fact broke down in tears. Having been a sniper in the Far East for a number of years, he'd never seen anybody survive leptospirosis and considered it a death sentence. With only about 80 per cent certainty about the cause of my illness, the doctors began to administer the appropriate antibiotic. My whole church, along with many others who knew me, were on their knees praying to God for my wellbeing.

During the critical time when the antibiotics battled against the disease, nobody knew what the outcome might be. Then after a few days, during the early hours of the morning, Joanne noticed a small amount of urine had seeped into my bag, an indication that my kidneys had begun to function a little. The doctors confirmed that despite being so perilously close to death, my condition had begun to stabilise. Joanne knew deep down inside that I'd turned the corner and might soon be on the road to recovery, and sure enough, I slowly moved away from death's door. After another week of intensive care, I was moved back into the isolation ward. Such had been my delirium that I thought I'd only spent an afternoon in intensive care, but it had been a lot longer. Each day, the nurses injected the antibiotic to kill off all trace of the disease and my veins ached with the continual bombardment. The doctors told me that leptospirosis is caused by a bacterium that germinates in rat's urine. If a person comes into contact with infected water, the disease can get in through the eyes, nose, mouth, ears, fingernails or cuts.

It was obvious I'd caught it whilst out canoeing with a group at work, but from the exact stretch of water I did not know. My guess was that it came from a canal in Chester, where I could remember swallowing dirty water after falling in while messing around. During the following week, I was visited by a continual stream of people who brought cards, gifts, food and well wishes. The fact that I couldn't go home, do any work or even look after myself properly released me into an unexpected period of peace that I'd hardly ever experienced in my life.

Each morning I watched the sun slowly rise across the Wirral countryside, dispersing mist from around the edges of the woodland as the autumn colours appeared on the trees. I wanted to remain captured in that existence for as long as possible, the peace was overwhelming. As I wondered about the exquisite peace, I remembered the words of Nicky Cruz's dad, which I'd read in his book, *Run Baby Run*. He described Nicky as a bird with no legs, always having to flutter around, never able to come to a rest. It described me to the core. Upon finding such perfect peace in that hospital room, I realised I'd never truly experienced it before. From my island of rest, I could see that throughout my life, my mind had never given me a moment's peace; it was always restless, hungry for more and ambitious. Even in the Christian faith I'd been running around, chasing, pushing and striving for one thing or another. That unexpected taste of luxurious peace made me realise that something important was missing.

...the experience of such peace came as
a result of escaping my busy mind...i
was completely free from its nagging...
not only that, as i edged away from
death's door, that peace became
very noticeable to those who came
to visit...there seemed to be a glow
coming from me...sublime peace...

...the exact same thing had happened
to me in grendon...while attached
to, and identified with the mind,
there was not a moment's peace...
but once i broke the dominion of
the mental ego, peace reigned...

...i was a long way from understanding
the full dynamic of what was happening...
but each incident shed a little more light...

It wasn't long before the doctors allowed me home again
and it was great to see my little Sarah; she hadn't been
allowed into the isolation ward where I'd been kept for
almost a month. While still convalescing, I got news from
Fairbridge Drake that one of the Trustees, Major General Sir
John Nelson, wanted to visit. I tried to put him off at first,
thinking it was a waste of time with me being so ill, but he
was adamant. Therefore, one afternoon as I lay on the couch,
the rough kids in the street looked on in amazement as a
chauffeur-driven Daimler cruised to a halt outside our door.

The chauffeur wisely stayed with the vehicle while Sir
John bounded in. Joanne and I didn't know what to expect

until a grey haired, strapping old gentleman entered the living room and flopped into a chair as if it were his own.

"Jimmy! Jimmy Rice, nice to meet you!" he said enthusiastically.

"Nice to meet you, too, Sir John. Please excuse me having to lie down."

"Oh, not at all. You carry on," he interjected. "Now, Jimmy, I've heard a lot about you. You're a man of faith, aren't you?"

"Yes, I am," I replied.

"Great news. Well done!"

He went on to ask how I became a believer and after a brief rendition, we talked nonstop for absolutely ages. We got on really well, striking up a friendship that I found very supportive for many years after. As a family, we visited and had holidays with him and his lovely wife, Lady Jane, at their home in Appin, Scotland. Many times, over the years, special people like David Fox and Sir John Nelson came into my life and brought a great deal of encouragement.

Following a couple of months' steady improvement, I set a date for returning to work, and in preparation, Joanne and I flew with Sarah to the Canary Islands for a sunny break. Having the heat on my back, swimming in the sea and generally running around served to lift my confidence for a return. Shortly after coming home, Joanne discovered she was pregnant again. We both wondered what it was about Spanish territory that brought these things on!

It was mid-February when I re-entered the office looking overweight, happy and as brown as a berry; everybody else looked pale by comparison. Such was the nature of my job, there could be no easy way back into it, no hiding places or taking a back seat. My personality wouldn't allow it anyway, so I got stuck in straight away and ran courses throughout the summer. Despite me appearing to do the job with my usual ease, as time went by I began finding it physically difficult; a problem I'd never known before. Sometimes while away camping with a group in difficult conditions I wanted to throw in the towel and give up.

Even with these difficulties, my life and work came more into the public eye. It came as a surprise to everybody to see me being interviewed by Roger Royle in the Albert Dock on national television. Standing alongside a beautiful sailing ship in a bright red sweatshirt looking strong and healthy, the story of my rise to success came across very powerfully. Over the weeks that followed, many people whom I hadn't heard from in years, contacted me to say how good it was to see me doing so well.

There were many newspaper shots of my team rock-climbing, canoeing or perhaps undertaking community projects, all designed to increase awareness and raise funds. On a national level, if the bosses in London gained a television opportunity, they invariably turned to me to do the interviews and I couldn't believe my luck – it was such fun. After getting to know a few of the film crews, they nicknamed me, 'one-take-Jimmy'. I had no fear of the cameras and could articulate our objectives without any trouble.

Following the Hillsborough disaster, I was doing a series of live appearances in Manchester for breakfast television, and bumped into the footballer Kenny Dalglish. We shook hands in the corridor and had a brief chat. He looked exhausted with all the funerals and grief he was having to deal with and I couldn't help but admire the endless work he did to help the victims' families. A number of my family members were at Hillsborough on that fateful day, including my younger brother, but thankfully they all came home safely.

Feeling increasingly weak as that summer wore on, my health began to flounder again. During the final course of the summer season, I had to rely upon Mick to supervise the group through most of the activities while I struggled in the background. It was very disconcerting not being able to function in my job properly. I didn't know which way to turn, because if I persisted and carried on, my health could become even worse. However, if I had to resign, where would I go? What would I do? Joanne was about to give birth to our second child and we had a house to run.

...it was a classic confrontation
between the negative, unbelieving
mind and trust in the realm that
assured me about my future...

...i'd been free for five years and found
the promise of 'it's all over, you'll never
go back to prison' to be wholly reliable...

...nevertheless, for reasons i could
not understand at the time, my mind
battered itself against those promises
and did all it could to undermine them...

...in later years, i was to discover that
the egoic mind is directly opposed to
the realm of consciousness/spirit...

...it's easy to proclaim faith in a place of
worship, or sit here and write of it in my
office while drinking tea, but i'm sure you
can appreciate, it was anything but easy
for me to hold fast in real-life situations...

...ultimately, my own mind proved to
be the most vicious and destructive
enemy i'd ever have to overcome...

It's curious how often I've prayed for something, but already knew the answer deep down inside. On that occasion, I asked to be given direction about which way to turn, within 24 hours; but somehow, I could sense it was already coming. In order to remain sharp and not miss a message when it came my way, I decided to go without food for a day. Most of the time passed without a whisper until in the evening I prayed again, thinking perhaps heaven had overlooked me.

This time a clear message arose. I was to listen to a tape recording that David Fox had sent to me two years previous. After initially doubting whether I'd been guided to listen to that particular tape, I played it anyhow. Having never heard to it before I wondered what was coming. It was a sermon all about how heaven brings a man through a problem. The speaker kept his focus upon just one subject, 'Going back into the fire.' Suddenly I didn't like the sound of it. As the cassette tape reeled along, it became abundantly clear that the message was for me to 'go back into the fire,' which meant going back to my job. Work had become so synonymous with pain, discomfort and frustration since my illness that the term 'fire' seemed highly appropriate. Joanne came in and sat alongside me while I listened.

"What's it like?" she asked.

"Stupid," I said.

As we sat together, I knew the message would become as clear to her as it was to me – there was no escaping it. When the tape finished I stomped up and down, annoyed.

"This is stupid," I said. "If I can't do the job, why do I have

161

to go back? What's the point? Doesn't heaven realise that I'm sick and can no longer do the work?"

Joanne sat quietly while I vented my frustration, but was surprised at what I said next.

"But, okay, okay, I'll go ahead and do it," I said, "no matter how stupid it looks, I'll go back. I asked for a message and got one. It's up to heaven now and not my fault if it all goes wrong."

> ...it's almost painful to read of the
> dilemma i was going through...
> on the one hand i had abundant
> faith, but on the other my mind
> literally went to war against it...

> ...if only somebody could have
> explained those dynamics it would
> have been a great help...but i had
> to figure it out for myself...

The mind is a wonderful servant, but a terrible master. Consider this: the mind can only exist in 'time' and is therefore blind to everything heading its way. At best, it makes fear-based calculated guesses about what may happen next, all of which are rooted in insecurity. The very best thing we can do for ourselves in this life is refuse to allow the mind to rule our lives, because it is utterly incapable of living in peace. Perhaps you may be wondering, "If I step outside of my mind, who runs the show?"

I hope my story, both in this book and the one that follows, will demonstrate that there is a reservoir of 'eternal life' inside every one of us that wants to help. The only think blocking its abundant flow is the mind that keeps a firm grasp on all the controls.

◆ ◆ ◆

Before returning to work I visited my doctor to tell him of the sluggishness that was plaguing me.

"You're fortunate to be alive Mr. Rice," he replied. "I don't know how you pulled through. It'll take a couple of years for your body to recover from the battering. Take a month off, then when you've finished that, take another."

His words made me feel more confused than ever. First, I was urged to return to work, now I was to be signed-off sick; where was the answer? The only solution was to keep letting go of what I 'thought' and trust the process.

When the answer came, it was almost comical. Whilst off work, I wandered into the church and joined the administrator, John Green, in his office for a cup of tea. After chatting for a while, he offered to pray for my situation, but as he was speaking the telephone rang.

"It's for you Jimmy," he said after picking up the receiver.

"Me?" I exclaimed. "Who would call me here?" It must be Joanne, I thought.

"Jimmy, I'm terribly sorry to trouble you at church," said the distinctive voice of Peter Lewis, the Director of our charity in London. It felt totally bizarre hearing his voice in that situation.

"That's okay," I said, wondering how he knew where to find me, let alone what the number was? I didn't even know it myself. He went on to explain that, after a considerable difference of opinion, (meaning a huge argument) my boss Dougie had resigned from his job and left the office, never to return.

"I just want to keep you in the loop," said Peter. "You're the senior man at your end. If anybody needs support, direction, whatever, please oblige – there's a good chap."

"Yes of course," I replied.

What an incredible turn of events! Peter and Dougie had locked horns on many occasions, but this time it must have been a bit special. Nevertheless, it was all well and good Peter asking me to support people, because in reality, I was employed as an outdoor pursuits instructor, not the Team Manager. I went home and told Joanne the news, and we were both sad to hear that Dougie had gone; he'd always been so good to us. We prepared some lunch and sat talking about the whole thing when the phone rang and it was Peter Lewis again. He never contacted me at home, and certainly not at the church, so this was once again very surprising.

"Jimmy, have you ever considered stepping-up to become the Team Manager yourself?" he asked, getting straight to the point.

His question caught me completely by surprise. "No, I haven't Peter," I answered. "I don't think it's really for me."

"Why's that Jim?" he pressed.

"Well, I feel confident about filling the role as it stands, but with all the new developments I've heard that are being added to the role, I couldn't cope with them."

"Which developments do you mean Jimmy?" he asked.

After detailing them, he interrupted and assured me that the Directors had decided against making any such changes.

"Oh, I see," I murmured, slowly realising what was happening.

"Will you come to London for a chat?" he finally asked.

With all of my excuses for refusing the position swept away, I suddenly felt energised for this new challenge. This time I'd be going to London not to compete for a job, but to be coaxed into one. What a deal! As with previous occasions when we needed faith to get through a tight spot, Joanne and I were thrilled with the answer. It was almost hard to believe. The Manager's position brought better wages, much more time at home with the family, and with a new baby arriving, it was perfect timing.

As ever, I had to go out for a long walk and clear my head. Something about the assurances I'd been given about my life kept shoving obstacles out of the way and opening doors for me. The experiences I was encountering were quite different from those I was learning about at church. My life was filled with grit, mistakes and adventure; but everything at church seemed very sanitised and under the strictest control. I was no expert, but those who were respected as having the highest religious virtues appeared fairly dull and lifeless to me. As a young family, we adopted valuable standards from the church regarding parenting, marriage and wholesome living, but when it came to raw faith, I needed little help at all. As time went by, Joanne and I relied upon ourselves in terms of where life took us; we needed little help from outside.

With regard to my new job situation, there was hardly time to celebrate before Joanne gave birth to our second child. Quite conveniently she went into labour just after Sarah had fallen asleep, allowing us to call the babysitter and disappear off to the hospital. Within a few hours she gave birth to our second daughter, Billie-Jean. It had been a relatively straightforward delivery, which went a long way to wiping out the memories of Sarah's troubled arrival. Like Sarah, Billie-Jean was in perfect health, weighing in at one ounce lighter than her sister at 8lb 8oz.

With all the turmoil of recent weeks out of the way, I decided to take up my new position straight away. Only four years had passed since I walked in off the street and was offered an instructor's job, and now I was running the show. As with the Team Leader's job, I began the Manager's position with slight trepidation. I missed the presence of my predecessor and wondered whether I could really hold it all down. However, as the days rolled into weeks, I got the hang of things and began to enjoy the job immensely. We were given notice to move our operation out of the building we had used for many years, so my first major task was to relocate the base from Birkenhead to Liverpool. It was a big upheaval for everybody.

As the move coincided with the end of the year, we decided to throw a big Christmas party where we could celebrate the old and usher in the new. Dougie accepted our invitation to attend, which gave everybody a chance to say goodbye properly. The biggest cheer of the night went up when we presented him with a gift.

In the new year, we moved across the river into a temporary base on Liverpool's dock front, while awaiting the conversion of a ship that would become our new floating centre. It took a whole year to complete but when it was finished it looked great with its office on the deck and a hall below. It also had a kitchen, storerooms, staffroom, toilets and showers. After some keen persuasion, we got permission to base ourselves on the quayside of the prestigious Albert Dock complex. It was a prime site, exposing us to the business community from whom we needed sponsorship. It was also easily accessible on public transport for young people all over Merseyside.

Besides offering a relevant service for hard-bitten young people, we built up a very good team who genuinely cared about the work. I managed to raise a lot of new funding, kept our team in the public eye and opened two new centres; one in Wirral, and helped start a whole new team in Salford. Just like the Instructor's job, and Team Leader's after that, being Manager stretched me to the limit, fulfilling all my potential over an exciting three-year period.

During that time, I received a visit from a social worker called Chris, who was concerned for a young scallywag under his care. As we talked he explained how he did voluntary work with Prison Fellowship, a Christian organisation that worked to help prisoners, ex-prisoners and their families. With my background, he must have viewed me as an ideal candidate for joining the Prison Fellowship support group he headed up. However, despite the passage of years, anything to do with prisons still made me feel uneasy; seeing the Risley bus in the mornings was about my limit!

As time went by however, I became more interested. The group he led were really nice people, so I went along and soon became a member. Chris knew I'd done some hard time in Borstal a decade previously, and therefore asked whether I'd go back and do a talk. I agreed without really thinking about it. Whenever I was asked to speak to groups of young people, I usually just said yes and got on with it.

On the evening Chris was due to collect me for the drive, uncomfortable memories of tough times ran through my mind. I still didn't like to share my feelings with people; therefore, as my anxiety grew, I covered it up and chatted as if nothing were amiss. Two hours later as we drew near our destination, my stomach twisted into a knot. I was distinctly uncomfortable. Old forgotten faces popped back into my mind, along with haunting memories of fights, aggression, and many weeks spent in solitary confinement. For me, Borstal spelt misery in every sense of the word.

Arriving a little early, we parked near the gate-house and passed the time.

"What's it like seeing this place again?" asked Chris.

"Not bad," I lied. "It's just a bit weird really."

I remembered hating everybody in the place, screws and lads alike. The only member of staff I was ever amenable to was Mr. Jupp. It was hard for me to understand why I liked him and not the others – maybe it was because he was a friendly guy; but then again, I'd hated plenty of friendly people too.

While I sat there thinking, an officer appeared at the gate, and as he stepped out to walk away I recognised him immediately.

"That's Mr. Jupp isn't it Chris?" I asked, opening the door to get out and say hello.

"Do you mean to say that you know Roger Jupp?" asked Chris, looking surprised as we stepped out of the car.

"Hi, Roger," said Chris, getting his attention, "Nice to see you again. How are you doing?" After they had shaken hands, Chris turned to me.

"Do you remember this fellow, Roger, about 10 years ago?"

Roger looked puzzled, his mind racing back and forth across his memory of the countless faces he'd come across in the job over the years.

"Rice," Chris suggested.

"Rice? Oh, yes, Ricey!" The memory came back in a flood. We stood talking for a few minutes, laughing about old times and characters we could remember. Then it was time to go in.

Seeing Roger like that was a real blessing and helped cushion the impact of my return, making it a little easier. Going back inside was a very strange experience. Everything seemed smaller than I remembered, yet by the look of it nothing had been changed. The chapel was a new experience for me. I'd never been near it while serving my sentence, not even at Christmas.

One of the lads who came to listen to my talk, lived near my house, and had become well known to me after completing one of our courses at work. He was one of those characters for whom going to prison was an essential part of the image he wanted to construct. Looking at his shaven head, tattoos and confident swagger, it was like seeing a piece of my own past.

"What could I say to help them back on to the right

track?" I wondered. Many young people press the destruct button and there's nothing anybody can do to stop them. All you can do is keep the friendship going and hope they show a desire to change before it's too late.

Mark Twain, the American writer, once wrote, "When I was a boy of 14, my father was so ignorant I could hardly stand to have the old man around. But when I got to be 21, I was astonished at how much the old man had learned in seven years." And that pretty well sums up the journey through teens!

During the meeting, the only thing I could do was stand up and tell the honest truth, and urge them that no matter how deep the quagmire they were in, there was a way out. "However," I said, "you have to be brave enough to admit that you've got it all wrong and seek help. Nobody can help a man who does not want it."

The meeting went quite well, but the chance for discussion was cut short by lock-up time for the lads. On our return to the gate-house, I was amazed to meet a few officers who remembered me from years ago. They were very surprised that I'd made it in life and seemed a little reluctant to come too close. Nevertheless, we a had a short chat before it was time to go, but before leaving, Chris asked them, "How bad was Jimmy in those days?" The four officers stood in a huddle for a brief chat and then said, "He was one of the top three worst offenders we've ever had. We still talk about him to this day. But it's nice to see things have turned out well."

During the return drive, I found their assessment quite a shock. I knew I'd been bad, but not that bad. Chris kept turning to glance at me,

"Top three worst, hey?" he said, smiling. "What the hell did you get up to?"

"I don't know Chris, it was a long time ago and I don't really think of it anymore."

Chris and I made a number of visits to speak in various

prisons together for a couple of years, although my availability was restricted by the demands of my job. It was my involvement with Prison Fellowship that bought me into contact with a man who became a friend, Noel Fellows. He was the main speaker at a dinner I'd been invited to attend in Liverpool.

His story was a harrowing one of injustice. He'd been interrogated, charged and convicted of a killing he knew nothing about. As an ex-policeman, he was given hell by the prison population for the duration of his seven-year sentence. It wasn't until several years after he'd been released that the real culprit for the crime was discovered, but by then the damage to Noel had already been done. He remained imprisoned in bitterness, fear and complete emotional turmoil until one day he had an encounter with God, which set him free.

During his talk, Noel skated over a subject that caught my attention that night – the issue of trust. He said that after the police, courts, his barrister, the jury, prison staff and prisoners had utterly let him down, all trust had been broken. Noel went on to say that the only person he learnt to trust was himself. He relied on nobody else.

15 years had passed since I'd run away from home and in that time, with the exception of Joanne, I'd found it very difficult to rely upon anybody but myself. Even when it came to being assured of my future by the 'true life' that arose from within, it was up to me to be strong and trust it; nobody could help me with that.

After five years of living in Paterson Street our growing girls needed more space and I wanted them to have their own bedrooms; therefore, we decided it was time to find a bigger house. Six eventful years had elapsed since I'd received the message to stay within those streets. Many times, I'd wanted to run away but had held on by the skin of my teeth. We didn't plan to move out of the vicinity of my learning, but began searching for a property more on the fringes of the neighbourhood.

It may seem innocuous, but at that time people who rented were looked on as fools; buying was the big trend. We'd fallen into the same way of thinking ourselves and never considering anything other than using the profit from the sale of the first house to buy a bigger one. Unfortunately, there was nothing in our price range that was suitable, as they were all located in the sort of places we were looking to get away from.

In the end, we simply broke with the idea of buying and decided to rent something that suited us as a family. I didn't like the idea of having to live in a place I didn't like just for sake of the property ladder, but I wanted my kids to have the best. That decision brightened our outlook and lifted a heaviness that had been pulling us down. At that time, a simple but profound message arose from the realm within that I came to know as 'true life': 'I'll give you the choice, worry or don't worry!' The implication was that I could simply let go of worries and ignore them.

"Okay," I said to myself. "I'll do it. I let go of the idea of buying a house and finding a rental as from this moment."

Shortly after, we stumbled on a beautiful house that had all the space and facilities we needed. We'd found it without any struggling and striving. However, the day before moving, I had to wait in the new house for the gas-man to arrive and connect us to the supply. As I sat in a comfortable chair looking out through the patio doors into the back garden, fear swept over me like a wave. A vindictive voice came nagging into my mind, ridiculing my decision to rent and undermining the life we were trying to live. "What have you done? What's happened to all your security? You're a fool. Everybody'll realise how stupid you are when you fall on your face. If you lose your job, you'll also lose your house. Then your family will have nothing. What king of husband and father are you?"

As I wrestled with those terrible thoughts, the memory of how I'd been 'attacked' on the eve of my driving test crept back into my mind. Reeling from this similar attack as it stabbed at my emotions, I managed to drag myself out of the chair and began fighting back until the doubts had been driven out of my system.

...as you can see, whenever i tried to
move forward in life, i came under attack
from my own mind...the problem was that
i knew nothing about the negative nature
of it, or the false identity of the ego...

...however, I was starting to understand
that my true inner 'self' could repel
the attacks, and that's what I did for a
number of years...the best way to learn
how to win those fights was to stop
sitting around moaning and fight back...

Not long after moving into our new house, Joanne and I began receiving the impression through prayer and meditation that we would soon be 'moving out into a new land'. It's very difficult to explain where such guiding messages came from, except to say they were not the product of the mind. For me personally, they emanated from a reservoir of life within; a life of loving assurance. When it speaks, I quietly 'know.'

We'd always looked forward to the day when the Birkenhead phase of our life was over in order to settle somewhere more permanently. The same kind of feeling came over me as I walked along the dockside during lunch-hour one day. Both my grandfathers had worked in industries essential to the heartbeat of Liverpool. One of them built ships in Cammel Lairds shipyard all his working life, while the other spent his time sailing those same ships across the seven seas. Such identity with the strength of the city, and the opportunity to contribute to its welfare through meaningful employment was a privilege missing in the lives of many people of my generation. But as I looked at those historic docks on that sunny day I realised I'd laboured at the very core of it. I'd worked hard and contributed much to the social needs of the day. "I can leave this city soon," I said to myself. "I've touched its heart."

CHAPTER 12

Entering a New Season

With my life having been transformed for over eight years, I became tired of beating a path from the jungle of my past into the future. Instead of being an ex-con, ex-fighter, ex-drunk or ex-anything, I just wanted to be the new man that I was. It was difficult to gain a clear perspective on what I'd become while still surrounded by the environment that spawned my wild behaviour in the first place. Such rumblings are natural, similar to those of a teenager wanting to leave school or perhaps a student nearing the end of degree studies.

"Is there change in the air, or is it just wishful thinking?" I wondered. The only way to find out was to put one foot in front of the other and see what the coming year held.

Things began with a trip to the United States to visit my old friend David Fox whom I'd first met when he visited my house with Mario from the Operation Mobilisation ships. I'd promised to make the journey after keeping in touch, but in truth I'd been reluctant to travel through fear of being rejected by immigration owing to my criminal record. Nevertheless, strong within my spirit was the assurance I'd been given when my life changed in prison: 'All things that had been lost have been restored.' Therefore, the prospect of making the trip became a challenge to me – could this promise break me through the concrete laws of immigration?

I knew full well that I wasn't allowed to enter the United States with such a criminal record and that I'd first need to visit the US Embassy and gain special permission. However, to my thinking, if the force of eternal life had already said yes, who could say no? With this promise comes the power. Therefore, I bought my return ticket to Pittsburg, via JFK in New York and went for it.

During the flight I felt quite relaxed, reading a book and chatting with various passengers, however the atmosphere changed as the jet entered Canadian airspace and headed south along the coast toward New York City. All of a sudden, the flight attendants walked throughout the plane handing out visa waver forms to all non-US citizens. When I looked at the form, it asked six simple questions, all of which needed to be answered in the negative, with a big 'X' in a box. One of the questions asked whether I'd been convicted of crimes and imprisoned. As all the other passengers bustled in excitement about their imminent arrival in 'The Big Apple', I disappeared into one of the toilets to think about what to do. As usual, my mind attacked me with its fearful point of view, and I had to battle hard to shove its ideas away.

"Should I lie?" I wondered, looking at the form.

To answer 'yes' to the criminal conviction question would be patently obvious, as there were six big boxes that were clear to see; not only that, I knew that details of my life would pop up on their computer system.

"Tell the truth," something inside me seemed to say.

After taking a deep breath, I ticked a big 'Yes' in the box pertaining to convictions, put the form back in my pocket and went back to my seat. This was it, crunch time.

After disembarking, I followed the swarm of passengers as they snaked their way down into the immigration hall. My nerves started to get the better of me as we inched forward, and there were moments when I wished I'd never made the trip at all. Gladly, with the arrival of other incoming flights, the immigration queue was quite long, giving me a chance to compose myself before the big moment. Once again, the nagging voice of my mind kept pecking away, telling me I'd be refused and humiliated; it took all my determination to dig deep and defy its voice. Then all of a sudden, with only a handful of people in front of me, an amazing thing happened; all my fears completely evaporated.

"Come on," I said to myself. "Take me to any booth. I'm coming through!"

It was such an incredible change of internal atmosphere that I don't think I'll ever forget it. It was as if 'fear' had fought me all the way, and then finally realised it had lost the battle, packed up its weapons and gone home.

Eventually, after being called to stand at a counter, I handed over my documentation and waited while the official checked my details. I was as calm as can be as he scoured his computer screen and wondered how on earth I was going to get through. Then, after what seemed an age, he turned ever so slowly in his chair, looked me in the eyes, broke into a smile, stamped my passport and welcomed me to New York.

"Enjoy your stay, sir," he said, and I could hardly believe it.

A lady tried to make conversation as I collected my case, but I was so desperate to get out of the baggage hall and breath the air of America that I completely ignored her. It was a very emotional moment for me; I couldn't help but recall all the years in prison thinking my dreams had been lost. True life had arisen from within me and said, 'Everything has been restored,' and now I was experiencing the reality.

After catching my connection to Pittsburg, I was met by David and his daughter Joyce. Seeing him on his own soil was quite strange, a real departure from years of communication centred around the streets where I lived. We drove through the darkness in his large comfortable vehicle, which was like a luxury mini-bus, across the State line from Pennsylvania into Ohio, and onwards to his home in Akron. Meeting David's wife, Faye, was a real pleasure as we'd only spoken on the phone a few times.

After supper, I headed off to bed, but despite having been awake for almost an entire day, I couldn't sleep a wink, such was the excitement of being in the US. The next morning, David and I left early to attend a service at his local church, 'The Chapel'. Don't be fooled by the impression given by the word chapel as it was a huge, multifunctional building with 8,000 visitors every Sunday. Some chapel!

We sat alongside David's friend Jack, who insisted upon buying breakfast afterwards. The whole morning was a lot of fun. Upon returning to the house, Faye had a beautiful lunch prepared for us, and thus began the biggest pig-out I've ever had over a two-week period in my life. American portions are enormous!

During my visit, we drove up past Buffalo to see Niagara Falls, which is magnificent, then across the border into Canada to Toronto. We stayed in a big hotel and met up with some of David's friends who had flown south from working with indigenous communities way up north. As usual we ate out in a restaurant, this time a pizza parlour. I was fascinated to hear all about the culture of the northern tribes.

On the return drive, we crossed the border further west at Sarnia to spend a day at the Henry Ford museum in Detroit. It was a fascinating place that not only displayed the entire history of American automobiles, but also lots of historic farm equipment. The most bizarre feature, which stopped me in my tracks, was the very car in which President Kennedy was shot in 1963. The traumatic newsreel I'd seen so many times since childhood, played once more in my mind. What a contrast to see such a piece of modern history sitting so quietly; almost forlorn. The story surrounding it seemed to set it at odds with the rest of the museum.

Finally arriving back at David's farm was something of a relief, as I was exhausted from all the travelling. Not being much of a touristy person, I'd have been content to poke around the local community or walk through the fields of his farm. His house was situated among the thousands of fruit trees they farmed every year, and wrapped all around them were ancient woodlands. Since my time in hospital, I'd developed the habit of quiet meditation and often mulled over things that stirred in my spirit while walking through the trees.

It's curious how certain events stick in the mind. Besides standing inches from the car in which Kennedy was shot in 1963, I'd always had an interest in the Kent State shootings that occurred in 1970. Unarmed students had gathered to demonstrate against the Vietnam war, when suddenly 29 guardsmen opened fire, killing four and injuring nine others. I suppose the newsreels had shocked my 10-year old mind and made an impression. Therefore, it was something of an honour to visit the campus and remember those who had fallen.

Before my trip was over, we were given an impromptu tour of the Cleveland Browns' locker room and stadium by a guy called Whitey, who was the team 'towel boy'. After that it was a trip to the nearby NASA Space Centre where I met astronauts, climbed in rockets and learned some amazing scientific facts.

It was a thoroughly fascinating trip, not just because of all the places we visited, but the massive lesson I'd learned about overcoming the opposition of the mind at the immigration desk. People talked about the devil as an external opponent, but to me, my biggest troublemaker was much closer to home. There was still a great deal for me to learn, but the more I put my faith on the line, the more I understood.

◆ ◆ ◆

The change that Joanne and I anticipated came, as usual, in a totally unexpected way. An actress called Penelope Lee had shot to public attention by directing a fascinating documentary based in Hong Kong called The Law of Love, broadcast in 1989. It told the amazing story of Jackie Pullinger, a young lady from England who made an incredible impact upon the residents of a crime-ridden place called the 'Walled City.' Living and working to help drug addicts, prostitutes, opium dealers and gangsters among the squalid population of 30,000, she did it all by faith, saving lives, breaking drug habits and setting people's lives back on the right track. Occasionally the Triads threatened to kill her, but in the end, even they were brought under her spell. It was an amazing story. Something about Jackie's faith awakened Penelope's, and that's how the documentary was born.

When filming was over, Penelope returned to England and asked people, "Can such a faith be found in our own country, where people really trust and have an impact?"

I've no idea how it happened, but somebody gave her my details, then one evening the phone rang and it was Penelope Lee herself on the other end. She asked for permission to follow me around with a microphone for a few weeks, and make a documentary for Radio 4.

Along with doing my job, I was speaking regularly all around the country, raising my little family and doing all kinds of interviews for radio and television. Therefore, to receive a request like Penelope's came as no surprise; that's the way life was going. Besides seeing her play a brief role alongside Marlon Brando in Superman and The Law of Love documentary, I didn't know much about her, but I agreed to the documentary nonetheless.

Joanne and I got on so well with her that she stayed with our family during recordings and we all became good friends. Change was still in the air for our family and Penelope was about to play a big part in the move. Having heard me speak at a meeting and the impact I had, she asked whether we would like to take a holiday to the village of Upottery in Devon where she lived. We would stay in an empty cottage she owned on the land. In return, I agreed to speak at a meeting of local young people that she had arranged.

With regard to the 'impact' I was having on groups and individuals, it was quite amazing, and to this day, I do not fully understand it. Sometimes I'd be halfway through a talk when an inner voice would say, "That'll do. Ask whether anybody wants to come forward." That's when all the unusual things took place, like healing, people falling unconscious, others crying hysterically, lives completely changed and spiritual blocks removed. It's no good asking me how I did it because I was as much a spectator as the audience.

The thing I learned to do was take no notes and just speak according to what arose in my heart. It was a scary practice to begin with, because people would have advertised the meeting and the hall would be filled with expectation. Upon being introduced, I'd be wandering up onto the stage without a message, and wondering whether one would arrive.

It usually went something like this: I'd start by saying hello and then I'd say, "Before I start, perhaps I could share something I can feel inside myself." An hour later it was all over and nobody ever remembered that I failed to go back to the proper 'beginning'. My attitude was that the reservoir of pure life within me knew everybody in the room, or at least what they needed to hear, and that was all I was waiting for.

As soon as the first few words arose from within, I'd speak them out and the rest came like a flood. Sometimes after the event, people had extraordinary things happen to them, and they would talk to me about what had caused it. But when they quoted me, they'd either quote something I'd never said, or they got it all out of context. So long as it worked, I didn't mind!

To me the explanation was simple, and prevented me from thinking I was clever and getting big-headed: it was the force within me that could reach people regardless of my words and without my understanding. Many times, when I got into the flow, it was as if I stood alongside myself and listened too, thinking, "Hey, this is pretty good." If I gave thought to what I was doing, I'd frighten myself to death, so I just kept going with the flow. Occasionally, if I was tired or under pressure before a big meeting, I'd start scribbling notes in the hotel room, but something inside would say, "Naah," and I'd have to throw them in the bin. I couldn't advertise healings, salvation, prophecy, life-changes or any of the other things that often took place, because I had no idea what might happen.

Therefore, having arrived in Devon, and Joanne pregnant with our third child, it came as no surprise when I made an appeal at the end of my talk, that every single child in the village responded. Some sat weeping quietly, while others became overwhelmed by the presence of a force that I can only describe as spiritual. It was a powerful meeting that spawned a whole new youth group that met each week for many years after.

Of equal significance to Joanne and I was the overwhelming impression that we should set our sights upon living in the village of Upottery. During the nine months leading up to the birth of our third and final little daughter, Ruby Joy, I was speaking publicly so often that the transition to doing it full time became inevitable. Having three young daughters was a responsibility we took very seriously, and that's why Devon, with its beautiful countryside became such an ideal location for us to raise them in.

◆ ◆ ◆

Nine years after being released from Grendon, we moved south and started a very different way of life. Being in a whole new environment helped me to look back upon all that had taken place since my release with a tremendous sense of satisfaction. Gone were most traces of the past, including the Risley bus in the mornings – to be replaced by a herd of cows that hurried by our cottage on their way to the milking parlour. The girls loved it.

Before long I was travelling far and wide, speaking to all manner of groups all over my country and beyond. Great things began appearing on the horizon, like being approached to write the first edition of this book, along with invitations to live in the United States.

Following the publication of the first edition of this book, Joanne and I made an appointment to visit the United States Embassy in London. We had been invited by some interesting people in New York to go and work among them for a few years. We had been in Devon for two and half years, had started home schooling our girls and life was looking good. However, as we drove along the motorway toward London, the usual fears began to surface.

"How can somebody like you, yes you, actually *live* in the United States?" said my ego, viciously. "You've got to be joking. You just got lucky last time, but now they are going to take a long hard look at you, and guess what, yeah, rejection." On and on… The attacking words were like arrows that had to be swatted away. Something inside me 'knew' we were heading in the right direction, despite the whole thing seeming to be impossible.

Accompanying us for the interview was the Pastor of our church, who felt like he needed to support our precarious petition.

"Who are you, sir?" they immediately asked him when we were called to face the officials. "Are you seeking a visa?"

"Well, no, but I er…"

"Please step away sir, you are not required," the official abruptly ordered.

As I handed our documentation across the counter, it was hard not to feel isolated, alone and fairly powerless. The cold facts of my life would be laid bare; I almost cringed as they reviewed our paperwork and studied their computer screen. Our application was for five two-year visas, one for each member of the family. Therefore, I almost fell through the floor when the official turned to me and said, "Here you are sir. We have issued each member of your family with a five-year visa.'

At that point, I wasn't hearing him too well, as my head was in a scramble.

"And if you desire to extend them to seven years," he continued, "please apply to the Embassy in Washington DC."

As we stood there dumbfounded, the official smiled, shook my hand, returned my paperwork and wished me a nice day.

After the enormous troubles of my younger years, I could hardly believe what was happening. Moving to Devon was quite a culture change for us, but travelling to America was more like the big leap forward I'd come to expect. Little wonder we had been discouraged from becoming bogged down in the housing market; we needed to be mobile and ready for this big change.

After three very enjoyable years living in the South West of England, our family of five boarded a jumbo jet from Heathrow in London and flew to Kennedy Airport in New York. It was to be my final attempt to envelope myself into the Christian church and its ways, but after two years I had to leave; it just didn't work out for me.

Curiously, the longer I remained in the West, spiritual concepts that were born in the East, such as Buddhism, became awakened within me. The biggest change sprung from the realisation that the realm of 'life' that I had discovered in prison, came from within and was not something to be sought without. I certainly wasn't trying to prove one faith right and another wrong; all I wanted was a truth that I could call my own.

During the five years we spent in the US, I travelled throughout the eastern States, speaking in many penitentiaries to thousands of prisoners. Along with that, I resurrected a Youth Court system for the County in which we lived. Basically, the Family Court system of New York was similar to British Magistrates. However, when it came to Petit Larceny or Misdemeanour cases, the court system was very slow to react – and that's where the Youth Court stepped in.

For example, if three teenagers were arrested for stealing CDs from a drug store on the way home from school, the detective offered the parents the chance to have the case heard in Youth Court. The condition was that they plead guilty, were tried by their trained peers and no record would be kept. Within a week of arrest, they would be cleaning fire trucks or performing some other community service – all of which was a lot better than waiting months for a Family Court hearing that may never actually happen.

It seemed so ironic with my background that I worked with local detectives, the Attorney's office, lawyers and the

Mayor, under the auspices of New York State Criminal Justice Department. I carried out lectures at High Schools, recruited volunteers and had them trained in real life court procedures. It was a great adventure.

Along with that, we home-schooled our girls for a number of years and I fulfilled many speaking engagements in Canada and Europe. It was a great experience for my children; I'd always wanted them to be unafraid of this world and taste as much of it as they could.

◆ ◆ ◆

When finally we decided to return to the UK, I couldn't help but think of the powerful impressions that had arisen from within me after my transformation. The first said, "This is over, you'll never go back to prison as long as you live." The second, "Everything that was lost, has now been restored to you." Both arose from what I came to know as 'the reservoir of life' within me, and both proved to be absolutely true.

EPILOGUE

While opportunities arose for me to spread my wings and speak all over the world from a Christian perspective, i continued to struggle with committing myself to a local church situation. Various groups invited me to join them in an attempt to add what i was doing to their portfolio, but after the initial warmth, my presence often drew jealousies and back-biting, and i couldn't be bothered with it. I think perhaps i was a bit too raw.

In some ways i felt guilty, as if my attitude was the problem and I needed to 'get in line'. However, whilst living in New York, i received a tremendous personal message that set me free from the whole thing. It was not unusual for me to have significant visions and dreams, they had been happening for years. The one i share with you now changed the way i journeyed through life and brought great relief.

My personal guidance came in a whole mosaic of different ways, usually without warning and rarely containing things i might have expected. On that particular occasion, the 'message' came from a persistent urge to find out about the life of the American Indian commonly known as, 'Crazy Horse'. I'd read thousands of books covering a wide range of interesting subjects in my life, many of which i'd been excited to get my hands on. However, the desire to find out about Crazy Horse was very different. I was pulled toward it from deep within, a place that nowadays i'd call, 'the reservoir of life.' A spiritual place.

Crazy Horse was an Oglala Sioux from the Black Hills of South Dakota, and was sometimes known as 'Ta-Shunka Witco,' or 'Curly,' or 'The Quiet One' – he never had much to say. As with all the young men, he was required to separate himself from his people and seek a spiritual vision for his life. A young warrior such as he could spend weeks out in the wilderness, fasting, praying and meditating. Once the vision was obtained, he would return and present his findings to the chiefs and elders. In Ta-Shunka's case, they agreed with the vision the young man had received and gave it their blessing.

The core of it entailed that he care for the old and infirm among his people, tending to their needs and offering them protection. In putting his people first, he never owned a decent horse, appeared very ordinary and always dressed simply. Known to be something of a recluse, he had little to say, was very modest, a mystic, fearless and a believer in destiny.

The years of his life coincided with the white man's push into the heart of the lands he had roamed all of his days. His courage brought him to fame as a fearless warrior, and during those desperate final years of resistance, his name steadily rose above all others. He was likely present at the battle of the Little Big Horn when, to the shock of the fledgling American nation, General Custer was slaughtered along with all of his men. It was to be the final act of significant defiance in the lives of the indigenous Indians.

Increasing numbers of troops were dispatched to either force the Indians to surrender or face being wiped out. The tribes had to split up and did their best to remain free, but it was a hopeless task. Many chiefs gave up without a fight, others succumbed to bribes, and large numbers of turncoats were equipped by the army and sent out to hunt their own people. Ta-Shunka led his people through the bitter winter, and unlike other chiefs, reportedly never once parleyed with the white man; he wanted nothing to do with them.

Rumours of his persistent defiance and ability to fight trickled in to the reservations and spread like wild fire, causing all kinds of unrest. Some of the chiefs became jealous of him, and claimed Ta-Shunka was harming their cause, while others were made to look upon their own surrender with bitter regret.

Another complication arose when the young warriors, looking to Crazy Horse as the hero of their peoples, began to despise their own Chiefs. Crazy Horse was adored, hated and feared in the reservations. Pursued by soldiers through vicious winter storms, the situation was eventually brought to a halt when 11 babies died in one freezing night; they could no longer carry on.

On May 8th 1877, the New York Times reported the surrender of Crazy Horse to Red Cloud's Agency, Fort Robinson in northwestern Nebraska. He came in to the reservation quietly for the sake of his people, and instead of milking the praise that awaited him, he pitched his tent six miles from the centre of the reservation, instead of the required three. Even the soldiers admired him.

It's hard to imagine the tension that arose owing to his very presence. Rumours spread of an uprising, holy men fuelled it with wild prophecies, soldiers were placed on high alert, the chiefs became furious with envy, and the young men spoiled for a fight.

Two leading chiefs, Red Cloud and Spotted Tail, circulated malicious rumours, splintering opinion about

Crazy Horse even further. The army and Indian chiefs wanted to get rid of him but feared full-scale bloodshed. While intrigue swept the reservation, Crazy Horse did nothing but live quietly as far away from the white men as he possibly could.

However, the spectre of his reputation hung so potently that the Army's Commanding Officer decided to bring him in for a parley. With tensions near breaking point, an unusually large party of Indian police were dispatched to make the arrest. Many of Ta Shunka's supporters rode along too, accompanied by others who spoiled for a fight.

As if things weren't bad enough, the Army chief was told that Crazy Horse intended stabbing him when they shook hands. A large crowd gathered as the big party of riders came to a halt inside the fort. Expecting to be escorted directly to the General's office, Crazy Horse suddenly drew back when it appeared they were going to lock him up in the guardhouse. In that moment of hesitation, he is reported to have produced a knife and cut the hand of the man who tried to restrain him. The tension was electrifying as the surrounding men eyed one another, weapons in hand: the whole scene was like a tinderbox, ready to explode into mayhem at any moment.

It was all too much for one young soldier named William Gentles, who snapped, and in a panic-stricken moment, bayoneted Crazy Horse in the back. As the warrior fell to the ground, he was heard to say to his close friend, He Dog, "I'm hurt bad."

With blood pouring from the wound, the young life of Crazy Horse slipped away in the night. Instead of the expected eruption of violence, most of the congregated Indians drifted mournfully from the scene.

As i finished reading that particularly sad part of the account, the following words arose from within.

"...and this is how young Crazy Horse was like Christ..."

Both lived at a time when their nations were under threat and rose to hero status just prior to their deaths. After spending a few years skirting around the edges of his nation, one of them made his triumphal entry into Jerusalem and was similarly greeted as a hero. But the tension his presence brought to bear upon the religious leaders, invading authorities and high priests was too much for them. Therefore, they conspired to butcher him. The people who had welcomed him so readily, chillingly changed their tune and cried for his blood.

Both of those young men carried a flame, a special glow. They were admired, fearless, young, mystical, kind to the poor and reclusive. When each of them finally turned inward to join their people, they were looked upon as torchbearers of a great collective hope. Nevertheless, in both cases that initial welcome rapidly turned sour and both ended up dead.

I'm not trying to suggest that those two young men were the same as each other, far from it. But through their lives, heaven delivered a personal message to me.

For years after i'd risen from my prison cell floor into a whole new life, i had associations with churches and religious groups. However, as hard as i tried, the relationships never worked out very well. All too often, groups had enthusiastically invited me to become a part of their organisation, only to turn cold. I just couldn't fold myself into the shape they wanted.

"Is it me?" i often wondered. It was a lingering question that remained unanswered for a long time. "Should i go back and dwell among them?" i wondered.

However, the issue became settled in a single moment as the stories of those two young men became fused together.

'Remain outside the camp.'

And that is what I have done ever since, choosing not to adhere to any one formal religion or set of rules, but listening to the true life that already exists within me, and being guided by that.

Printed in Great Britain
by Amazon